AFTA SpringerBriefs in Family Therapy

A Publication of the American Family Therapy Academy

Founded in 1977, the **American Family Therapy Academy** is a non-profit organization of leading family therapy teachers, clinicians, program directors, policymakers, researchers, and social scientists dedicated to advancing systemic thinking and practices for families in their social context.

Vision

AFTA envisions a just world by transforming social contexts that promote health, safety, and well-being of all families and communities.

Mission

AFTA's mission is developing, researching, teaching, and disseminating progressive, just family therapy and family-centered practices and policies.

More information about this series at http://www.springer.com/series/11846

David Trimble
Editor

Engaging with Spirituality in Family Therapy

Meeting in Sacred Space

AFTA
American Family Therapy Academy

Springer

Editor
David Trimble
Division of Psychiatry
Center for Multicultural Training in Psychology
Boston University School of Medicine
Boston, MA, USA

Boston Institute for Culturally Affirming Practices
Boston, MA, USA

ISSN 2196-5528 ISSN 2196-5536 (electronic)
AFTA SpringerBriefs in Family Therapy
ISBN 978-3-319-77409-1 ISBN 978-3-319-77410-7 (eBook)
https://doi.org/10.1007/978-3-319-77410-7

Library of Congress Control Number: 2018940505

Printed on acid-free paper

This Springer imprint is published by the registered company Springer International Publishing AG part of Springer Nature.
The registered company address is: Gewerbestrasse 11, 6330 Cham, Switzerland

Series Foreword

The AFTA Springer Briefs in Family Therapy is an official publication of the American Family Therapy Academy. Each volume focuses on the practice and policy implications of innovative systemic research and theory in family therapy and allied fields. Our goal is to make information about families and systemic practices in societal contexts widely accessible in a reader friendly, conversational, and practical style. AFTA's core commitment to equality, social responsibility, and justice are represented in each volume.

In *Engaging with Spirituality in Family Therapy: Meeting in Sacred Space,* David Trimble and the chapter authors step beyond the boundaries of usual clinical/professional discourse to open themselves to generative dialogue with each other and with readers. Chapter after chapter, the authors share their own journeys as self-reflective spiritual beings working with families. Representing diverse spiritual traditions and metaphysical practices, the authors describe how they simultaneously engage with clients' spiritual lives and their own experiences of the Divine.

It is impossible to read the book without being deeply moved and, in some way, transformed by the vulnerability and professionalism of the authors as they invite readers to move beyond thinking of spirituality as an instrumental characteristic of clients to viewing therapy as a potentially sacred space where multiple spiritual perspectives and experiences are honored and engaged. In so doing, they model inspiration for cultural transformation and challenge family therapists to consider how they may contribute to an ethical dialogical approach to spirituality.

Lewis & Clark College
Portland, OR, USA

Carmen Knudson-Martin

Contents

From the Margins to the Center: Generative Possibilities in Multicultural Dialogue on Spirituality 1
David Trimble

Family Therapy With Palestinian Arabs: Building on Inherent Habits of Spirituality for Psychological Well-Being 15
Khawla Abu-Baker

An Unknown, Unnamable Journey: Family Therapists in Complex Conversations as Muslim and Sikh Immigrants 33
Kiran Arora and Saliha Bava

The Gift That Keeps on Giving: Culturally Relevant Integration of Spirituality in Family Therapy With African American Families 49
Paulette Hines

Harnessing Spirituality Within Traditional Healing Systems: A Personal Journey 67
Hugo Kamya

The Tao As & Of Spiritual Healing: Reframing Reconciliation and Recovery 83
Jay T. King

Meaning Making Through Family Constellation Work 89
Linda Longo-Lockspeiser

Vision Quest: The Intersection of Native American Spirituality and Family Therapy 107
Rockey Robbins

A Conversation in Sacred Space 123
David Trimble, Khawla Abu-Baker, Kiran Arora, Saliha Bava,
Paulette Hines, Hugo Kamya, Jay King, Linda Longo-Lockspeiser,
and Rockey Robbins

Index.. 141

Contributors

Khawla Abu-Baker Alqasemi College of Education, Baqa Alqarbia, Israel

Western Galilee College, Israel

Kiran Arora Long Island University, Brooklyn, NY, USA

Saliha Bava Marriage and Family Therapy Program, Mercy College, Dobbs Ferry, NY, USA

Houston Galveston Institute, Houston, TX, USA

Taos Institute, Chagrin Falls, OH, USA

Paulette Hines Department of Psychiatry, Rutgers Robert Wood Johnson Medical School, Rutgers University Behavioral Health Care (Emerita), Piscataway, NJ, USA

Hugo Kamya School of Social Work, Simmons College, Boston, MA, USA

Boston Institute for Culturally Affirming Practices, Boston, MA, USA

Jay T. King Palo Alto University, Palo Alto, CA, USA

Boston Institute for Culturally Affirming Practices, Boston, MA, USA

Linda Longo-Lockspeiser Private Psychotherapy Practice, Valley Stream, NY, USA

Rockey Robbins Department of Educational Psychology (Counseling), University of Oklahoma, Norman, OK, USA

David Trimble Division of Psychiatry, Center for Multicultural Training in Psychology, Boston University School of Medicine, Boston, MA, USA

Boston Institute for Culturally Affirming Practices, Boston, MA, USA

From the Margins to the Center: Generative Possibilities in Multicultural Dialogue on Spirituality

David Trimble

Introduction: Why This Particular Book?

Spirituality is recognized as an important dimension of family therapy practice (Walsh, 2009). This book explores generative possibilities in a multicultural exchange among family therapists actively engaged as spiritual beings in our work. Drawing on Rivett and Street's (2001) distinction between "instrumental" and "metaphysical" family therapy practice, we know how to make instrumental use of our clients' own religious and/or spiritual practices in the service of healing. We are challenging ourselves to go further, sharing our own metaphysical practices as self-reflective, embodied spiritual beings working with families. How do we engage simultaneously with our clients' spiritual lives and with our own experiences of the Divine?

Family therapy affords its own lenses on an intercultural exchange about spirituality and religion. Family therapy began by expanding the lens of treatment beyond the boundaries of the individual, and continues to expand the lens to include network, community, society, culture, and the well-being of our planet. Family therapists' postmodern lens opens conversation to meanings that emerge in the "space between" participants in dialogue. We have sought that generative space in the conversations that shape this book.

I am grateful for this phrase from bell hooks' (1984) work on resisting the marginalization of discourses.

D. Trimble (✉)
Division of Psychiatry, Center for Multicultural Training in Psychology, Boston University School of Medicine, Boston, MA, USA

Boston Institute for Culturally Affirming Practices, Boston, MA, USA
e-mail: d.trimble@earthlink.net

D. Trimble (ed.), *Engaging with Spirituality in Family Therapy*, AFTA SpringerBriefs in Family Therapy, https://doi.org/10.1007/978-3-319-77410-7_1

This book is grounded in the belief that, without revolutionary transformation of human culture, life on our planet may not survive the activities of its dominant species. In the words of Chief Arvol Looking Horse (2016),

> We are now at the crossroads: Either unite spiritually as a global nation, or be faced with chaos, disasters, diseases, and tears from our relatives' eyes… Our vision is for the peoples of all continents, regardless of their beliefs in the Creator, to come together as one… thus promoting an energy shift to heal our Mother Earth and achieve a universal consciousness toward attaining Peace.

Chief Looking Horse's message resonates with the Messianic tradition of my Jewish faith, with the Christian Lord's Prayer's "Thy will be done on earth as it is in heaven," and with messages of hope for the world from the ancient traditions and recent revelations of many human cultures.

Humanity now has the means for nearly instantaneous and universal communication connecting us with each other, but the current global discourse embodying individualistic ideology is not well suited to the exercise of collective responsibility. Cultures are always in process of transformation. Could recognition of human spirituality and acknowledgment of the sanctity of all Creation be elements of an emerging human consciousness that respects the planet's ecological vulnerability, and rejects war?

Universal respect for spirituality is often obstructed by religious particularism, the claim that one's own religion is superior to others, or even the only acceptable Truth. Defense of perceived threats to one's religious faith remains a powerful motive for violence. Universal acknowledgment of human spirituality will need to celebrate the glorious variety of particular religious forms in which that spirituality is embodied, rather than seek hegemony for a particular form or ideology.

How to write about this topic when the multitude of belief systems and spiritual experiences make it so difficult to find a common language? For example, the words "experiences of the Divine" (employed above) embody a perspective that may be unfamiliar and perhaps alienating to some serious metaphysical practitioners.

The reader will encounter a range of constructions of spirituality, expressing multiple religious and spiritual perspectives. Some authors draw from the religious legacies of their birth. Others are seekers, pilgrims practicing metaphysically far from their original spiritual homes. In conversations among the authors, we have reached beyond the limits of our traditions and personal constructions of spirituality, to find in the dialogical "space between" moments of collective experience in which we have tasted experiences beyond the limits of language, space, and time. In the last chapter, we explore the challenges of bringing such moments of spiritual vitality into our clinical practices.

Addressing Exclusive Claims to the Universal

At the beginning of the twenty-first century in the United States, it has only recently become acceptable for therapists to talk about spirituality, expanding psychotherapy's range to include people for whom this dimension of experience is vital. The potential range of spiritually informed psychotherapy is, however, constricted by the silencing power of dominant discourse (Hare-Mustin, 1994). Although the United States Constitution permits the free exercise of religion, Christianity is that society's dominant religious discourse. Dominant discourse subtly shapes what is considered to be "true," "real," or "normal." When religious or spiritual ideas differ too much from the dominant Christian discourse, they may at best be marginalized, at worst forbidden in the practice of therapy. For several of the authors in this volume, their practices transgress the boundaries of the dominant North American religious discourse.

Permissible and Impermissible Beliefs

I count the following among permissible, Christian-informed UnitedStatesian "mainstream" beliefs: Love is a redemptive spiritual force. A soul that continues to exist after we die is incorporated in our physical bodies. The practice of forgiveness frees us from the pain of resentment and self-absorption. Living a moral life improves the quality of the human soul, with implications for its state of being after this physical life. God responds to our earnest search for God's presence in our lives. Remorse and repentance are redemptive spiritual forces.

Beliefs that are not as mainstream, but still permissible within a dominant Christian discourse, include the following: To the discerning eye, God's purposes manifest in the course of events in this world. People who have cultivated their relationship with God can achieve abilities to heal illness (Other people are simply born with this gift). The universe and God are one.

The following beliefs, which are coherent with many non-Christian faiths, I believe are impermissible within a Christian-informed dominant discourse: The soul undergoes a journey through multiple physical incarnations, culminating with direct experience of unity/identity with God. People who have cultivated their spiritual capacities can achieve abilities to project their consciousness beyond their physical bodies, through space and time. There are worlds beyond, yet interconnected with, the manifest physical world, for example, the shamanic worlds (including the animal spirit world and the world of the dead), worlds of energetic beings more evolved than human beings, and the *Kabbalistic* worlds of *Asiyah, Yetzirah, Beriah,* and *Atzilut*. Shamans and other practitioners can enter states of mind that enable them to travel in these worlds beyond, and to collaborate with companions from these worlds (e.g., power animals, spirit guides, Divine messengers).

Building a Redemptive Multivoiced Discourse

Reflecting on the challenges of cultivating a global discourse that respects human spirituality and offers an alternative to the individualistic dominant global discourse of neoliberal capitalism, I recognize that, whatever form this emergent discourse takes, it must embody both optimism and humility about human nature. As biological beings, we have been shaped by an evolutionary process that has fitted *Homo sapiens* to a scavenging, hunting, and gathering environment, in which members of small bands relied on each other for survival. One benefit of our evolution is that we are relational beings, "wired to connect" (Fishbane, 2013). However, one evolutionary consequence of small bands of ancestors competing with each other for territory poses a challenge for the development of a global culture grounded in universal human spirituality. A study of the effect on implicit bias of the "cuddle hormone" oxytocin, a neurohormone that evokes nurturance and intimacy (De Dreu, Greer, Van Kleef, Shalvie, & Handgraaf, 2011), suggests that, as we feel closer with members of our in-group, we are more prejudiced toward outsiders.

Human culture has enormous influence over the expression of human nature. On the one hand, neoliberal capitalism informs self-seeking individualism that overrides our relational interdependent nature. On the other hand, many if not most religious traditions, responding to the potential violence of human prejudice, claim a more universal message of peace for all humanity, even all Creation, expanding our perspective beyond our tribal nature. For example, in the Abrahamic religions (Judaism, Christianity, and Islam), one can trace over time in their texts deliberate efforts to reshape human nature. In the *Torah* of Judaism, Moses was the messenger for the practice of establishing sanctuary cities, protecting from blood vengeance individuals who caused accidental death. As the texts of the Jewish Bible evolved, the Law came to replace the impulse for personal vengeance. The Jewish Biblical injunction to "love your neighbor as yourself," including the stranger living in your land, was further universalized by Christianity to include all strangers in the world. The root of the very name of Islam embodies the Arabic word for peace. Yet, religious fundamentalism is currently a source of oppression and homicidal violence in the world. How can culture evolve to differentiate respect for universal spirituality from particularistic loyalty to one's religious tribe?

This book embodies the authors' collective efforts to express that respect, while still embodying the particularities of our spiritual understandings. It is a step toward a multivoiced dialogue regarding religious and spiritual meanings. The authors represent a range of cultural, religious, and geographical birth locations. As we wrote, we also engaged in conversation with each other. Our conversation was informed by the construct of dialogue articulated by Russian literary theorist Mikhail Bakhtin (Holquist, 1981), who could not afford to be explicit in his Soviet political context about his Christian faith, which appeared, disguised, in his reverence for The Word. Dialogue is a relational process. Meaning does not exist within the boundaries of the individual but is shaped in the space between the speaker and the listener. The speaker's utterance finds its meaning in the listener's response, which turns the listener into the speaker and the speaker into the listener, and so it flows, in an "unfinalizable" sequence. Dialogue is playful, generative, and intrinsically unpredictable. Its unpredictability can make it difficult to sustain when social injustice, intolerance, or personal injury prompt retreat into the safety of the singular discourse of monologue (Kamya & Trimble, 2002).

In contrast to dialogue is monologue, which expresses a particular idea, argument, or ideology with the intention of persuading, convincing, or imposing itself on the other. With some exceptions, most religious doctrines are monological in nature. Monologue is not intrinsically "wrong." Although it may represent a wary retreat from the messiness of dialogue, it can also be essential for the coherence required in philosophical, theological, or scientific argument. Many religions are by nature closed, self-referential systems of belief and practice that seek internal coherence and consistency. Our challenge as authors, which, we believe, resonates with the challenges for family therapists engaging with spirituality, is to be faithful to our own religious/spiritual selves as well as to the religious/spiritual selves of the members of the families in our consulting rooms. This is consistent with the family therapist's practice of connecting with all the members of the family, demonstrating that one can see through the eyes of each of the others in the room.

Our hope for this volume is *not* that we find some consensus on a universal discourse of religion or spirituality, but, rather, that we work together to create an ethical dialogical space in which to explore our different spiritual and religious experiences. A global culture that respects human spirituality cannot do so by prescribing a single monolithic religious discourse.

The authors bring to our conversation a variety of perspectives informed by Christianity, Islam, Judaism, Native American spiritual practice, Sikhism, Southern and Eastern African spiritual traditions, and Taoism. We were charged to consider the contradiction between the current dominant discourse of individualism, ill-suited to address problems of war and environmental degradation, and spiritual discourses of compassion and mutual responsibility. We were asked to reflect on the challenges of religious fundamentalism to the emergence of a global spiritual culture. Each author was asked to articulate her/his intersectional identities as a spiritual being in social and cultural contexts, to describe her/his metaphysical practice as a clinician and/or teacher, and to illustrate with examples of his/her practice. The final chapter shares some of our dialogical conversation across our differences, with particular attention to the relational ethics of the conversation between spiritual beings and the implications of relational ethics to emergent, global, spiritually informed culture.

Clinical Practice: Boundaries and Ethical Concerns

Using Rivett and Street's (2001) distinction between instrumental and metaphysical, *instrumental* use of spirituality in therapy involves helping clients draw on their familiar spiritual beliefs and practices to make constructive life changes when possible, and to find healthy ways to go on in circumstances beyond their control. Respectful and appreciative of their clients' religious and spiritual practices, therapists help clients put their practices to use in the service of healing. When practicing *metaphysically*, therapists engage in therapeutic conversation mindfully from their position as spiritual and religious beings in their own right.

Whether practicing instrumentally or metaphysically, therapists are careful not to impose their beliefs or practices on their clients. They do not indoctrinate or proselytize. They are careful not to assume that their religious experience is the same as their clients', even when they both profess the same religion and denomination (Griffith, 1999).

There is more complexity to ethical considerations in metaphysical practice. One's "qualifications and training" as a metaphysical being are embodied in one's religious, spiritual, and esoteric life, rather than in one's professional training. The rules for scientific psychotherapy are often different from rules for one's spiritual practice. Scientific knowledge, especially the method of inquiry, must be made available, but metaphysical knowledge may be closely held—the esoteric can be harmful to the unprepared or uninitiated. There may be a developmental spiritual mismatch between the clinician and the client; the client may be an "older soul" but less well-developed psychologically or less healthy emotionally than the "younger soul" clinician. The experience of awe can be seductive. Metaphysical practice involves powerful transcendent experiences that can challenge the clinician's ethical imperative to place clients' needs and experiences first.

I suggest the following set of ethical principles for spiritually informed therapy: The initial assessment includes exploration of clients' religious and spiritual experiences. Clients and therapists collaborate to develop a plan that may include instrumental use of clients' religious and spiritual resources (perhaps including help with their conflicts over accessing this domain of their lives). In some cases, it may appear that the therapist can be helpful by operating metaphysically. One's metaphysical practice is unique to one's own embodied spiritual experience. I have colleagues who operate explicitly as shamans, journeying on their own or in the company of their clients' spirits in nonmaterial realities. My metaphysical practice involves sharing intuitive knowledge that comes to me from realms beyond the material world. Whatever the particular form of the metaphysical practice, the therapist is obliged to operate consistently within the standards of that metaphysical practice, having trained with mentors and accountable to knowledgeable teachers, elders, clergy, masters, or whatever role is appropriate to the particular form of the spiritual/religious practice. The therapist remains mindful of both metaphysical and psychotherapeutic principles. When metaphysical and psychotherapeutic imperatives are in contradiction, the psychotherapeutic imperative always trumps the metaphysical.

The judgment as to when to seek informed consent for a metaphysically informed conversation requires humility and skill, as the therapist is asking the client to consider a new element in the therapeutic contract. Two kinds of judgment are called for. The therapist makes a clinical judgment as to the client's capacity to manage the potential disruption from introducing the possibility of metaphysically informed practice, and the potential benefit or harm for therapeutic outcome. The therapist has also has to make an informed judgment as to whether or not the intervention "makes sense" from a metaphysical perspective. For example, from within a perspective that sees the person as embodying a soul on the course of a journey through multiple incarnations, the therapist may make a judgment as to the "readiness" of the soul for metaphysical work.

Having explored these considerations, the therapist may seek clients' informed consent, explicitly locating her/himself as a spiritual being and asking permission to draw on metaphysical ways of knowing. Operating with informed consent, the therapist should be in regular, active consultation with trusted colleagues who operate comfortably with both psychotherapeutic and metaphysical discourses.

Locating Myself in My Journey

I am one of the seekers and pilgrims represented in this book; a heterosexual, White, English/Scots-Irish UnitedStatesian man early in my eighth decade, the scion of many generations of Christian Protestant Methodist ministry. I am a Jew—by denomination Reform, by theology Neo-Hasidic, a student of esoteric Jewish *Kabbalah* and *Chasidut*, learning to integrate my complex religious faith with a shamanic practice that predated my conversion to Judaism. Most mornings, I strap on head and arm *Tefillin,* ritual objects whose use in prayer has been required of observant Jewish men for nearly two millennia. As a Reform Jew, I respect the *mitzvot*, Divine commandments embodying the covenant between Jews and our God, and choose mindfully which to observe in these modern times. When I meditate, I concentrate on Hebrew liturgy and Scripture, and on the *Sefirot,* the pattern of Divine qualities that emerges from the limitless, unknowable Unity of *Ein Sof.* The *Sefirot* organize the forms of Creation from the highest nonmaterial realms to the material world. I meditate on their embodiment in my mortal being, using the capacity to direct metaphysical energies within my body that I cultivated as a student of Chinese *Chi Gong* earlier in my journey. As my consciousness ascends to higher realms, I seek to unify the material with the nonmaterial, dissolving distinctions between lower and upper realms, realizing the Divine purpose of Creation, which is awareness of its Source. As I cultivate my meditative practice, it enhances my capacity to travel as a shaman in spirit worlds.

The journey that brings me to this moment started with a childhood of obsessive and fruitless prayer. A terrifying childhood dream of Divine manifestation, abandonment, and demand for responsibility embodied a collision between my ancestral legacy of Call to ministry and my father's unspoken determination that no child of his would become a minister. My discovery of Buddhist meditation in adolescence restored my access to spirituality. In college, participation in the psychedelic revolution gave me direct experience of the Unity of Being that resonated with the ideas of Spinoza I encountered in philosophy class. Learning family therapy in graduate school led me to network therapy (Speck & Attneave, 1973), and thereby to my first spiritual Master, an *espiritista* who opened me to a direct experience of universal Divine consciousness. That brief moment of revelation enabled me to operate in shamanic mode conducting family network assemblies—gatherings of household, extended family, friends, neighbors, fellow congregants, and others with concerns about a family in crisis. It also inspired me to seek texts and teachers in traditions including Sufism, Buddhism, Hinduism, Taoism, shamanism, Hawaiian *kahuna,* and Native American spirituality, finding commonalities in the esoteric cores of many traditions. I found a second spiritual Master in a practitioner of Chinese medicine who taught me how to direct spiritual energy through my body using *Chi Gong*.

I came to Judaism as the husband of a Jewish woman who readily became a stepmother to my son and daughter from my first marriage, and I agreed that we raise the child we adopted together as a Jew. For years, I participated comfortably in Jewish life without intending to convert, as I continued on my own spiritual path. Over time, my familiarity with Jewish services transformed into love. I made the decision to convert when I sensed the presence of ancestors at Sinai during the Torah service. I delayed conversion, first so as not to upstage our son Jacob's Bar Mitzvah, later because of the struggle to help him make his way through his difficult adolescence. When it became apparent that there might not be an end to his struggles with mental illness and substance abuse, I began serious study for conversion. After a couple of years of study, the date of my formal conversion was delayed for several weeks, so as not to take place within the traditional 30 days of mourning after Jacob's death at the age of 19 from driving while drunk and manic.

Broken-hearted, I found myself communicating with Jacob's spirit within minutes of his death, entering the spirit world with him and accompanying him for a week until I observed his spirit dissolving into the One, his soul a drop returning to the ocean of *Ein Sof.* His soul returned to me weeks later, and has remained near to me since, sometimes accessible when I seek him by projecting my consciousness into the spirit world, sometimes appearing unbidden and powerfully present. My search to make sense of these phenomena led me into explorations of *Kabbalah* and *Chasidut,* which are now at the core of my current Jewish meditative practice. Two years after Jacob's death, meditating deeply in the manner that I described earlier, I realized that I was building at that moment my capacity to accompany his soul, a capacity that 2 years earlier had seemed to come to me out of nowhere. Time is not necessarily linear in the upper worlds.

Developing Spiritually, Practicing Metaphysically

When I practice metaphysically, much of what I do does not fit the model of spirituality implicit within the dominant North American religious discourse. In addition to using a conventional diagnostic lens to make sense of new clients' needs, I employ a metaphysical lens to perceive the evolutionary stage of their souls. When clients are open, willing, and able to collaborate in direct metaphysical conversation, we speculate together about the deeper meanings of events in their current incarnation. I may share what may "come to me" from my spirit companions as we seek to discern design behind dreams, coincidences, and apparent happenstance, helping clients to understand themselves as spiritual beings, to consider life choices, and to interpret their experience. I began my explorations of *Kabbalah* and *Chasidut* more than a decade ago. The more I develop my Kabbalistic meditative practice, the better I am able to practice shamanically, projecting my consciousness beyond the material world. As I have consulted with knowledgeable Rabbis, ethical considerations have become more complicated for me. Not all of my emerging abilities are appropriate to offer in the context of a service that I provide for a fee. Although I always see the world through the lenses that I have cultivated as a spiritual being, I maintain a boundary between my clinical practice, which is strongly influenced by my spiritual practice, and specific shamanic practices of seeking to influence material reality by petitioning in nonmaterial realms. This distinction is particular to me, in the context of my practice as a Jew as I understand it, chosen with Rabbinic consultation, but not a distinction that I wish to impose on others. I have enormous respect for colleagues whose shamanic journeying is an explicit aspect of their psychotherapeutic practice, and many of whose patients seek them out specifically because of that specialization.

I do practice nonremunerated healing outside of my professional practice. When I practice as a healer by petitioning in the upper worlds, I am always guided by the words of Lakota shaman Black Elk (Neihardt, 2008), words that I had incorporated into my teaching of network therapy decades ago:

> Of course it was not I who cured. It was the power from the outer world, and the visions and ceremonies had only made me like a hole through which the power could come to the two-leggeds. If I thought that I was doing it myself, the hole would close up and no power could come through. Then everything I could do would be foolish. (p. 163)

Within the domain of my professional practice, I find myself working more frequently with advanced souls embodied in troubled and vulnerable human beings. These cases require that I find practical strategies to deal with the metaphysical problem of evil. From a *Kabbalistic* perspective, advanced souls in troubled bodies are vulnerable to parasitic attacks from *kelippot*, or "husks." The husks are so distant from their Creator that they lack any spark of the Divine light that bathes Creation in God's loving regard. They try to rise upward by draining spiritual energy from beings who are closer to the Source, dragging themselves and their victims further from the light, as a drowning person tries to climb toward air by pulling down the rescuer.

From a perspective that sees everything to be a manifestation of the Divine, the husks are neither good nor evil. They are necessary elements of a design that affords human beings with the ability to choose, and part of the cyclical process of exile and redemption that is integral to Creation's evolving consciousness of its Source. From the perspective of an immediate situation with a suffering patient, I understand the husks to be malevolent spirits who are causing harm. Although I actively protect myself from their influence, it is not my place to engage them directly to protect my patients. I must help my patients learn to protect themselves.

Sympathy for the Devil: The Case of Gracia

When I met Gracia, I recognized an advanced soul embodied in a suffering patient. Through my spiritual lenses, I saw that her soul had, over the course of countless mortal incarnations, achieved spiritual refinement that brought it closer to its Divine source than most human souls. Yet, in this life, the accumulated effects of multiple emotional injuries overwhelmed her. Raised in Europe by parents and grandparents traumatized by the ravages of the Second World War, a remarkably intelligent girl taken from school in sixth grade to care for younger siblings (a deep loss that, now in her sixties, she still mourns), she left home and country as a young woman to live with her new husband and his parents in the United States. She described emotional and psychological abuse by her mother-in-law that continued from her husband after they established their own home with their young children. Experiencing her mother-in-law as embodying unrelenting evil, Gracia set her mind not to become angry and resentful like her. Although she had grown up skeptical about the Catholic Church of her youth, Gracia set her mind to become a devout Christian. Her parish priest, Father Tom, was a lifeline for her. Temperamentally a generous and caring person, Gracia drew on her faith to cultivate herself further, and was comforted by her deep love and adoration of Jesus.

Gracia came to my office originally for treatment of her 10-year-old son. As her son improved, we began her own psychotherapy, for complicated psychological and emotional challenges including traumatic stress disorder and somatization. A gentle, sensitive, and caring person, she radiated spiritual light. It was clear to me from the beginning that, for all that she was limited in this life by her history and symptoms, her soul was far more advanced than mine along its journey of return to the Source. I offered her the choice of allowing me to practice metaphysically in the course of therapy. She understood, and freely gave her informed consent. When I referred her to my *Chi Gong* master to treat her somatic symptoms, he also recognized her as someone of great attainment. I learned that Father Tom was working in parallel with both of us. Gracia had heard about the Self-Realization Fellowship, a spiritual community founded by Yogi Paramahansa Yogananda. She approached Father Tom with some trepidation to see if a visit to their meditation center would violate her Catholic faith. He enthusiastically endorsed the venture, telling her that he himself had attended an SRF Retreat! Father Tom's esoteric practice went far beyond the limits with which he felt his Bishop, if he knew, would be comfortable. Father Tom's "readings" included stories of Gracia's past lives with her husband and mother-in-law. Members of the Self Realization Fellowship also recognized Gracia's spiritual qualities, and invited her to study their esoteric teachings.

Radiant souls like Gracia's are like beacons in the spirit world, attracting both benevolent and malevolent spirits. Benevolent spirits had guided her to Father Tom, who could fully appreciate her advanced spiritual nature, help her within the frame of reference of their religion, and support her exploration of the Yogananda community. Her spirit guardians led her to me, a therapist who could appreciate her for who she was and also treat her emotional and relational injuries. On one occasion, she had a vision of Jesus appearing to her as she drifted into sleep, vivid and unmistakably present as he gazed at her with profound compassion, weeping tears of blood. Terrified that she had become psychotic, she had in me a therapist who could treat her with respect as someone with the genuine capacity to experience such visions.

Even as Garcia had guides who led her to vital supports, she found herself in situations that drained her spiritual vitality. Over time, she developed the strength to build a life for herself beyond self-sacrifice in her relationships with members of her family. A pattern emerged in which, at nearly every step of her personal emancipation, she would become overwhelmed by misfortune—hit by a bicycle and sustaining a head injury while walking, just as she was about to return to the skilled work that she had set aside to raise children now grown, sideswiped as she drove her car on the eve of taking a job after her slow recovery from the first accident. Gains in psychotherapy would soon be followed by toxic emotional demands from her adult daughters, for whom she still felt responsible because they had seen their father abuse her when they were children. She appeared trapped in a pattern—whenever she would take a step to liberate herself, she would be brought down, describing herself as drained and complaining of physical ailments that restricted her from supporting herself independently.

Through metaphysical lenses, I could see her radiance build and fade. I offered her a frame within which to make sense of the pattern, using the image of her radiance in the spirit world drawing predatory parasites to her. Although she was aware that I was a Jew, she knew that I respected her Christian perspective. I talked of Satan as a jealous adversary who was resisting her spiritual growth, and encouraged her to protect herself. I counseled her to protect herself carefully whenever she was making gains, as Satan was most likely to strike when she was taking a step toward her liberation.

I was fully aware that my interventions could be intelligible from a narrative therapy framework as using externalization to help her to sustain gains whenever she was leaving the familiarity of habitual self-limitation. I also knew that I was authentic and sincere in believing my own words, as I translated my *Kabbalistic* understanding of the struggle between benevolent and malevolent spirits over a radiant soul into Christian language and metaphor.

This intervention had at best modest effect. Although she could see the pattern, and was aware of her vulnerability, it was very difficult to enlist Gracia in an adversarial struggle with the spirits who were draining her vitality. Her generosity of spirit, her instinctive compassion, and her reluctance to cause another being distress were all virtues at the very core of her being. They contributed to her vulnerability to exploitation, her fragile sensitivity to others' pain, and her difficulty asserting herself in her family relationships. Determined to find a way to help her protect herself, I decided to enlist Gracia's virtues. Drawing heavily on the imageries of both *Kabbalah* and the Christian story of Lucifer's fall, I explained to Gracia that she was contributing to Satan's misfortune! I told her of the long journey that Satan needed to take to reunite with God, having fallen so far and keeping himself so estranged from God by the evil that he was doing. Whenever she let Satan succeed in draining her energy,

Gracia was obstructing Satan's redemption, diverting him from repentance and adding to his guilt. Startled and mildly amused, Gracia quickly grasped what I was saying. She indeed became better able to shield herself from malevolent greedy spirits, sending them away with compassionate concern for their redemption. Rather than becoming debilitated every time she took a step forward, she enjoyed the cumulative building of her strength. This became the template for understanding what she needs to do to separate from her husband. She has come to understand that she will only be able to send him away when she has built the strength to tolerate her own empathetic heartbrokenness over his feelings of abandonment and loss.

Souls Engaging Across Differences

Sheila, my sister, was a Tibetan Buddhist. A few months before she died of lung cancer, she asked that I arrange one of my visits to coincide with a weekend workshop on the Tibetan Buddhist approach to death led by Andrew Holocek and convened near her Oregon home. I read Holocek's book (2013) before the visit, gaining knowledge that helped explain my late son Jacob's ongoing presence in my life. I learned how, from the perspective of Tibetan Buddhism, the prayers of the living can help the soul make it through the *Bardos*, states of transition including and beyond the death of the material body. Some souls may emerge from travel through the *Bardos* in a Pure Land, in which they continue to evolve in encounters with other advanced souls, and from which they can witness and communicate with loved ones in the land of the living. I was struck by the resonance between esoteric Judaism and Tibetan Buddhism. The Pure Land of the Buddhists resonates with the Garden in *Kabbalah,* a place of sojourn for the souls of the righteous. Just as a Pure Land is created by a Buddha to welcome evolving souls, so the God of Israel delights in the souls of the righteous in the Garden.

I kept my promise to pray for Sheila in her journey through the *Bardos*, even as I was confident that she would make her way. The *Rinpoche,* or leader, of her religious community, a distinguished Tibetan monk, sent her word before she died that he would guide her soul along its journey. My daughter, Jessica, herself a Tibetan Buddhist, was also praying for her. About 3 weeks after Sheila's passing, Jessica and I both sensed that Sheila had made her way to the Pure Land.

Jessica and I had a rich conversation about this experience, in the process each of us elaborating on our particular understandings of the soul's journey. Both of us deeply grounded in the discourses of our respective spiritual traditions, we honored the resonance between our ideas and also the distinctions between them. We respected that each of us was drawing on the discoveries of meditators, visionaries, and prophets in our traditions, and that both traditions had their unique approaches to making sense of phenomena beyond the reach of mortal awareness. In Rivett and Street's (2001) paradoxical language, we appreciated "the same and different and the same." I witnessed our creating a sacred space (Kamya, Chap. 5) between us, and also within our own hearts, without reducing one discourse into another, or seeking to invent an overarching discourse to subsume them both. It came to me that a global culture that respects universal human spirituality must acknowledge the multitude of particularistic forms in which spirituality is expressed.

In the pages that follow, I invite you to enter the sacred space between you, the reader, and the authors as they share the particularities of their practices. I believe that family therapists can make an important contribution to the development of an ethical dialogical approach to spirituality. My own early family therapy training led me to work with larger and larger contexts as a network therapist, and my religious practice envisions a God both beyond and within all that exists. I appreciate the paradox that my religious understanding, all-encompassing and universalistic as it may be on its own terms, is too restrictive for an emerging global human discourse that must embrace all forms of human spiritual practice.

In my view, family therapists offer more to this global conversation than readiness to look beyond the immediate situation of the psychological individual. Our field incorporates its own variety of discourses, among them readiness to engage with complexity, humility about the limitations of any claim to truth, courage to maintain a stance of not knowing, and respectful readiness to engage in openhearted dialogue. I hope that you will find in these pages inspiration for your spirit, and opportunity to make your own contribution to the evolution of human culture.

References

De Dreu, C. K. W., Greer, L. I., Van Kleef, G. A., Shalvie, S., & Handgraaf, M. J. J. (2011). Oxytocin promotes human ethnocentrism. *Proceedings of the National Academy of Sciences, 108*(4), 1262–1266.

Fishbane, M. (2013). *Loving with the brain in mind: Neurobiology & couple therapy*. New York: W.W. Norton.

Griffith, M. E. (1999). Opening therapy to conversations with a personal god. In F. Walsh (Ed.), *Spiritual resources in family therapy* (pp. 209–222). New York: The Guilford Press.

Hare-Mustin, R. T. (1994). Discourses in the mirrored room: A postmodern analysis of therapy. *Family Process, 33*, 19–35.

Holquist, M. (Ed.). (1981). *The dialogic imagination: Four essays by M.M. Bakhtin. (C. Emerson & M. Holquist, Trans.)*. Austin, TX: University of Austin Press.

Holocek, A. (2013). *Preparing to die: Practical advice and spiritual wisdom from the Tibetan Buddhist tradition*. Boston: Snow Lion.

Hooks, B. (1984). *Feminist theory: From margin to center*. Troy, NY: South End Press.

Kamya, H., & Trimble, D. (2002). Response to injury: Toward ethical construction of the other. *Journal of Systemic Therapies, 21*, 19–29.

Looking Horse, A. (2016). *Important message from keeper of sacred white buffalo calf pipe*. New York: Indian Country Today. Retrieved October 15, 2016, from: http://Indiancountrytodaymedianetwork.com/2016/08/26/important-message-keeper-sacred-white-buffalo-calf-pipe.html.

Neihardt, J. (2008). *Black Elk speaks: Being the life story of a holy man of the Oglala Sioux (the premier edition)*. Albany, NY: State University of New York Press.

Rivett, M., & Street, E. (2001). Connections and themes of spirituality in family therapy. *Family Process, 40*, 459–467.

Speck, R., & Attneave, C. (1973). *Family networks*. New York: Pantheon Books.

Walsh, F. (2009). *Spiritual resources in family therapy* (2nd ed.). New York: Guilford Press.

Family Therapy With Palestinian Arabs: Building on Inherent Habits of Spirituality for Psychological Well-Being

Khawla Abu-Baker

I received my training as a couple and family therapist in the United States. During that period, I worked with American as well as immigrant families. Some of them were Arabs from the Arab World, and some Palestinians, citizens of Israel or the Palestinian Authority.[1] It was obvious to me that cases of Arab clients[2] reverberate with their original culture, including the religious and spiritual norms they carried. I recognized that special attention has to be paid to the clients' context of religiosity and spirituality, as important components of their cultural background and daily life.

---

[1]The terminology that describes Palestinians reflects one's political attitude about the Israeli-Palestinian conflict. Other names are used include Israeli-Arabs, Arab-Israelis, minorities in Israel, Non-Jewish citizens, among others. This chapter will use the terms, "Palestinian citizens of Israel," or "Arabs," according to the context (for further reading on this issues, see Rabinowitz & Abu-Baker, 2005). Since daily life in Israel is highly influenced by Jewish laws, religious and other aspects of the lives of Muslims, Christians and Druze citizens are highly influenced by politics.

[2]Arabs live in the Middle East and North Africa in 22 countries, or what is also called the "Arab World" – all share the same culture, language and history. Palestinians are Arabs; some of them (1.2 million) live as citizens in Israel; 3.5 million live in the Palestinian Authority and the rest (about 10 million) live in other Arab countries or in the Diaspora. Most Arabs are Muslims. Christians make up about 10–15% of the Middle Eastern population and about 9% of Palestinians in Israel while Druze areapproximately about 1% in the Middle East and about 8% in Israel.

K. Abu-Baker (✉)
Alqasemi College of Education, Baqa Alqarbia, Israel

Western Galilee College, Israel

D. Trimble (ed.), *Engaging with Spirituality in Family Therapy*, AFTA SpringerBriefs in Family Therapy, https://doi.org/10.1007/978-3-319-77410-7_2

Islam as the Compass of Arab Culture

Arabs adopted Islam when it was established in the year 622. Since then, Islam has influenced Arabic culture and language and saved it. The Quran, the holy book and the constitution of Muslims, is written in Arabic, and all prayers should be conducted in Arabic for all Muslims in the world.[3] The Quran saved classical Arabic as an ancient Semitic language. Islam forms and organizes the believers' thinking and how they experience life.

Arab Muslim, Christian, and Druze communities of the Middle East frequently turn to spirituality in times of stress and loss, integrating it harmoniously within daily life. Spiritual practice may be marked by symbols such as dress code, tools, or special language, engaging family and community support in times of need. Spiritual rituals are designed to help people confront and digest stressful events, learn from them and find new meanings. Their main goal is to gain a sense of collaboration in managing the stressful event with the supernatural power[4] *Allah*/God, that, it is believed, caused it in the first place. Spirituality thus empowers people who feel helpless and powerless.

This chapter emphasizes the contributions of religiosity and spirituality to psychological well-being for Palestinians. It shares examples of using spiritual intuitions of national/political or personal tension, uncertainty, danger, sadness, fear, and loss. It introduces the idea of combining internal motivation of the client with an external locus of control (religious belief). This chapter suggests implications for therapy and social mental health for the benefit of students, practitioners, and other professionals who are interested in the influence of religion, culture, and politics on daily life of Palestinians or in the Arab World.

The next section introduces a case study that will be analyzed and used in several sections throughout the chapter.

Case Example

Nuha was a 25-year-old single Palestinian woman, a citizen of Israel. She adopted Western dress code and secular lifestyle, had obtained an academic degree, and worked in her family business. Nuha used to pray the five daily obligatory prayers Muslims should maintain and was fasting once a year the whole month of Ramadan. She sought therapy for feeling depressed. In the session, Nuha hesitantly revealed that 3 months prior to starting therapy, she was possessed by an "evil soul" *roh sherera*. She suffered from constant abdominal aches, sequential tantrums, uncontrolled crying, and loss of weight. Over the course of 2 months, she was hospitalized twice for her severe abdominal aches. Doctors were not able to diagnose the reason

[3] About 2.2 bilion

[4] Allah is the Arabic name of God. Muslims believe that it is the same God of Adam, Noah, Abraham, Ishmael, Isaac, Moses, Jesus and Muhammad.

for her pain. Her sister, an ultrareligious Muslim who covers her head and face with black veil (*Niqab* or *Borkah*), suggested that Nuha start a treatment based on religion.[5] Nuha moved to her sister's house and got special therapy based on Islamic principles led by two Muslim clergy *sheikhs*. The ritual included reciting special verses from the Quran three hundred times each, twice a day, while also maintaining the five-time regular prayers and listening to the Quran for the rest of the day. This therapy plan was kept as a secret from Nuha's parents and other nonreligious siblings. Nuha explained the need for secrecy as "People think that this kind of therapy using religion is primitive and not useful. Since I don't veil and don't dress up as a religious Muslim woman, people don't believe that I'm spiritual and very religious. Even I was afraid that you will misunderstand me and misjudge me."

I was aware of Nuha's concerns. Most people in my society do not accept both this and lifestyle, specifically when the dress code of Muslim women does not fit the lifestyle she declares. Also therapists, mainly those who were trained in Israeli or Western institutions, relate to therapy practices reliant on religious beliefs as "naïve" or "primitive" or "influenced by placebo effect"(Arieli & Aychen, 1994; Endrawes, O'Brien, & Wilkes, 2007; Sengers, 2003).

Therapy with Nuha proceeded with total acceptance of integrating my therapeutic work and the spiritual/religious therapy. I showed interest in the procedures she was still practicing in accordance with the therapy plan of the two *Sheikhs*. I suggested to incorporate relaxation and directed imagery tools while citing verses from the Quran or while praying five times a day. As a family therapist, learning more about the practices of therapy using Islam helped me be acquainted with Nuha's family dynamics including power relations, secrecy, issues in consensus, and fanatic ideas. I related to the "evil soul" as terminology Nuha used to express her experience. A few months later, Nuha was able to flourish and carry out her life plans without any physical pain or psychological stress.

What made Nuha hide the special spiritual/religious therapy from her family and hesitate to share that experience with me as her therapist?

In order to introduce the comprehensive answer to this simple question, one should enlarge the focus to see the influence of larger systems on Nuha's life. The policy of the Israeli regime relates to religious Muslims as a resistant movement who maintain ideology against Israel. Members of the Islamic Movement in Israel relate to secular Muslims as "non-believers." Nuha's religious sister belonged to the Islamic Movement. Her norms, dress code, lifestyle—including her relation with her husband—all were influenced by their special version of interpreting Islam. Nuha wanted to blend her western lifestyle with her Islamic/spiritual ideology. Had she declared that she was a devoted Muslim, she would face suspicion from two directions: (a) the Israeli authorities for her Muslim religious belief system and (b) by her society for her Western lifestyle. In order to protect herself, she practiced her spiritual and religious life secretly, losing the community support aspect of common worship and spirituality. Nuha lived in a type of double bind: "You are damned if you are religious and if you are not!".

[5] For further reading on this issue see Hussain (2011).

Thinking, Language, and Locus of Control as Constructed Belief System

It is uncommon to be "purely" secular in the Islamic Arab world. According to Shouby (1951), language reflects a way of thinking and social relations. An Arab person, Muslim, Christian, or Druze, uses the name of God countless times a day as a part of their thinking system. When a religious Muslim prays five times daily, then he or she mentions the name of God at least a hundred times. In addition, the name of God should be mentioned in ordinary daily life acts such as before preparing dough or food, before eating, when entering an empty room or dark place, as an opening to all prayers, as a protection from Satan before sexual intercourse, preceding a speech, and before closing a business deal. All these religious practices penetrate daily life and are highly adopted among religious and secular Arabs from all religions in the construction of their traditions.

Additionally, the presence of God exists intensively in Arabic language due to codex of social politeness. A person should wish the partner in the conversation pleasant wishes that ask God to make a decision for the benefit of that person. According to religious belief, a Muslim should not plan any step in life without asking God to support that plan. *In shaa'Allah,* translated literally as "if God permits," is used by Arabs as "yes I want" in order to let God's decision lead theirs. This notion is influenced by the belief that people's lives are controlled by God's decisions.

I became aware of the depth of the presence of God in Arabic language during my studies in the USA. I was amazed to discover how many times during a short conversation an Arab pronounces the name of God. It starts with the greeting question "how are you;" its answer should include the sentence "Praise God" *alhamdu li Allah.* The full answer could be "I'm feeling very good, Praise God" or "I'm feeling very sick, Praise God." When during the conversation, the speakers have a decision, they should include the sentence *bi ithin Allah* "if God allows" or *in shaa Alla* "if God permits." Between these opening and closing sentences lives a culture that relies on God as the responsible guide, comforter, and master of a person's life. If a person answers to the first question "how do you feel" by "great, everything is fine, I'm doing very well," Muslims believe that soon God will put that person in a suffering experience so he or she would learn that they are not masters of their lives, rather the guardians. If a person decides regarding a plan without adding the sentence *in shaa'Allah* if God permits, then unexpected obstacles will prevent that plan from being achieved. This language reflects a culture that is influenced by Islam as a faith that teaches that the locus is external and it is held in the hands of God.

When Nuha became disturbed, she was in a crossroad in her life where she felt that her plans were exploding in her face one after the other. When her physical pain exacerbated, and her sister had diagnosed her by having "evil soul" in her body, she explained all events as "a message" from God. Among other issues she had discussed in therapy with me, she wanted to find a flow path where she could be guilt-free while combining her own form of religiosity, spirituality, and secular lifestyle.

Nuha's need was familiar to me as I myself grew up in a family and community that were totally secular and had moved gradually to diverse kinds of religiosity and fanaticism.

I had to create a plan where Nuha had to be self-motivated to cure her complaints, and synchronize that with other belief system in where she believed that God's plan was to help her cure. So her belief in her inner motivation should support her belief in the external locus of control in her life. One may think that the two belief systems are contradictory, or encouraging her to adopt helplessness. Often times Western trained therapists try to teach Muslim Arabs to learn to be self-motivated and self-responsible and shift to internal locus of control (Ghorbani, Watson, & Khan, 2007; Yousef, 2000). This one-sided intervention can at best only be partly successful, because a full adaptation to it means that a person would believe that he or she could plan and fulfill all their wishes without God's help, thought that is considered as sinful—a notion that could cause serious psychological and social problems.

I will share the process of socialization to Islamic lifestyle in my own family of origin as a psychosocial and political narrative of a family that shares the same cultural background as Nuha's.

Heritage and Religious Socialization

In Arab societies, people inherit their ascribed religion, then some of them chose it as their lifestyle and their identity through the education and socialization process they go through (Peek, 2005). School curriculum in most of the Arab and Muslim countries teaches Islam lessons as a philosophy and as a daily practice. The Arab media have some specialized channels for teaching Islam and the lifestyle of Prophet Muhammad. The education system and socialization process cooperate to raise Muslims to adopt Islam as their constitution and way of being. Not all Arab Muslims adopt the five obliged pillars of Islam or practice the daily obliged prayers or choose the Islamic dress code. However, the components of their individual, family, and social norms are rooted deeply in the Quran and *Sunnah*. For example, people who believe in the Quran and *Sunnah* without practicing any of the worship may consider themselves as "traditional believers." Some other people fast the month of Ramadan or pray on Fridays in the mosque as a family or community tradition more than as a religious practice. When Muslims are devoted in practicing all obliged pillars of Islam on a daily basis, including dress code, they would be considered as religious Muslims. It is expected that at different stages in their lives, Muslims choose the degree of their commitment to their religiosity and spirituality. Muslims are not allowed to convert to other religions or to be atheist (Ghorbani et al., 2007).

I was born to a Muslim traditional family. In the early years of 1960s, as a young couple, my parents, like other Palestinian people their age, maintained a combination of modern and traditional lifestyle, and similar attitude toward religion. My parents' dress code was Western—an influence of the British Mandate on Palestine, as was their educational plan to provide equal chances for their female and male children. According to the traditions, my mother and all her six children had to obey the father as the male and the elder. We used to fast the whole month of Ramadan. None of us were committed to the five-time daily prayers. Instead, my father used to pray in the mosque the Muslim prayers for the high holy days. Similar to my parents at that period, most other Palestinians in my small town related to themselves as traditional—not "religious." A small community of few families who belonged to a Sufi order lived in a courtyard adjacent to their own mosque and maintained their daily prayers and weekly ceremonies. Their female elders covered their head with white long chiffon shawls while all others adopted western dress code. They were a visible religious community in my small town.

When I was born, the Palestinian society in Israel was still suffering from the post-trauma of the 1948 *Nakba*, when Palestinians lost their homeland; properties and coherent families were torn between Arab countries, where they lived as refugees. New regime, new language, new dominant religion, and new lifestyle were imposed on Palestinians who remained inside the borders of what became the state of Israel.

The private Catholic school Terra Sancta was very close to our house. My parents, as many other Muslim families in the old city of Acre, decided to send their children to gain good education and concrete discipline in the Catholic school. Religion as school discipline was not among their concerns.

Annexed to the school stood a small monastery with a small church that was established in the year 1217. Catholic priests from Europe lived in it and served Christians in the holy land—Terra Sancta. When I went to school, priests from Italy and Scotland lived in the monastery, led the mass on Sundays, and directed the school. In comparison to our home that, at that time, did not include any Islamic symbol or accessory, the monastery and church were decorated with rich icons and statues for Jesus, Mary, and other saints; the priests themselves, in their brown long gowns, were a kind of living Christian symbols.

Islam does not allow drawing portraits of God or Prophet Muhammad due to a cultural concern that aims not to compromise the unity and transcendence of God (Esposito, 1988). The ban became absolute and was extended to any representation in art of the human form for fear that such statues or paintings might lead to idol worship.

As a child, it was difficult for my imagination to create a picture of Prophet Mohammad, while the statues and pictures of Jesus around me helped me to empathize with his short yet full life.

Multiple Narratives in Religions and in Family Therapy

In my private Catholic school, Christian students had a mandatory religion class while Muslims had a free time. In third grade, I asked for a special permission to attend the class in order to hear stories about prophets' lives. I was totally hypnotized with each story that described relations between individuals, emotions, mind, family, community, and God. At that age, I was not able to differentiate between myth and reality. Oftentimes I left the class full with tears for sympathizing with a person or more in each story. My experience in that class acted as a winch that drew me to become interested both in relationships and in the spiritual world.

When I was in fifth grade, we started having classes about Islam. The curriculum of teaching Islam as a subject at elementary school focused on the philosophy of Islam, learning by heart verses of the Quran, studying obligatory prayers, and gaining knowledge about faith and rituals of worship.

Stories about Prophet Mohammad and his family were very sad. His life included loss, orphanhood, and detachment from several parental figures. I had to imagine Prophet Mohammad and his family and friends in different periods of his life and create a portrait of him that suited his persona. The goal of teaching his story was to follow his life path and adopt his ideas, wisdom, and ways he practiced life and Islam. That is the *Sunnah'*.

In sixth grade, I started to pray five times a day and tried to veil—without success. It was under the influence of the fear I accumulated from the description of the "doom's day" and the "judgment's day" I learned in the classes. During that period, I was busy thinking about the type of relation that has to develop between me, a small girl, and God, the Mighty. Beside the fear, I knew that the development of this relation was taking the wrong way. I do not remember how long this period had lasted: days, weeks, or months. My family had not supported nor rejected my acts. However, in my surroundings at that time, a young person who became religious was judged as "backward."

In ninth grade, and for the following 4 years, I learned Judaism, mainly *Torah, Mishnah, Talmud*, and "*Perkee Avot*" as part of the Israeli curriculum for Palestinian schools. In those classes, faith, language, narratives, history, and politics influenced the interpretations of the text and oftentimes caused heated discussions regarding the national subtext. Now that I had already studied three religions, I experienced constant comparisons between religious narratives. Four years in high school were a type of preparation for my later training in family therapy when I learned to listen to multiple versions of the same story and to accept the presence of multiple realities for couples and families as for religions and nations.

The next section introduces two ideas: (a) adopting religion and spirituality as a way to deal with loss and trauma and (b) conducting worship practices as an opportunity to experience "open access" with God that allows undeviating monologues directed to him. These two ideas help people in distress to feel helped and guided. The section also offers examples of the connection between major life events with various practices of religiosity and spirituality for secular, traditional, and religious Muslims.

Trauma, Loss, and Spirituality

Prayers and Religious Monologues as a Therapy

My parents became devoted Muslims after the death of my sister, their first-born, at the age of 25 years. The day she went into deep coma for 10 days before her death, she let the people who surrounded her bed know that female deceased relatives whom she mentioned by their names were visiting her for the last week and had promised to accompany her in her last journey. She had described their white shining dresses and the light of their aura. Few tears dropped from her eyes, not having energy for more. My sister, who never related to herself as a religious person, asked us to read loudly verses of the Quran, since that was a therapy for her headaches. No one asked questions. I believe that we related to her at that moment as the "esoteric knower"—this person who was moving back and forth between this life and the afterlife. I believe that we did not have the terminology to form proper questions for that type of rare conversation.

In the ninth day of diving deep in coma, a day before my sister's death, my father had a dream where my sister asked him to pray for her and to become closer to God himself. My father was sure that what he had experienced was not a dream rather a real talk between him and his daughter, who was between the two forms of life. Since that day, religion, spirituality, and traumas have influenced my psychological development and my family's, in various ways. The death of my sister transformed our relationship with her from what we were used to, to a new relationship with what we experienced as "her spirit." Embracing religion and spirituality became (a) the only possible source of remedy to the injured souls caused by the trauma of death and (b) the way to continue having a relation with her in her new form as "a spirit."

Oftentimes a trauma causes individuals or families to "become religious" or to "hold for their Islam." The loss of beloved ones, and thinking about their spirits, makes people engage in spirituality, some during the mourning period and others for the rest of their lives.

After the death of my sister, my parents related to religion in different ways: My mother adopted Muslim dress code and veiled, became spiritual, prayed the obligatory five prayers, and prayed many voluntary prayers in order to spend more time in the presence of God. She also prayed for the previous years that she was not devoted. After the prayer, my mother used to negotiate and bargain with God regarding the health, life, success, and happiness of her children. Becoming devoted helped my mother to have a direct relation with God, who, she believed, is taking care of her daughter. She used to say to God "you sent her to me and you took your present back. Now, keep the rest of my children and take me before you take any of them." Oftentimes, these crying out monologues *Monajat* ended with uncontrollable tears. This direct speech with God let my mother calm her agony. The prayers functioned both as a spiritual encounter and as therapy for her grief. My mother extended her religious education through some reading and by watching some specialized TV channels.

My father focused on the sociability of the religiosity. As a man, he prayed in the mosque, a practice that kept him social, and brought him to be a member in the Islamic council in his town. Praying in the mosque, not alone at home, kept my father away from falling down into depression.

My mother used to praise herself that she never asked God "why he decided to take her daughter. Instead she used to say "praise God, '*alhamdu li Allah*' he took my daughter." Muslims who blame God put themselves in an equal position that enables them to criticize—an act that is considered as a sin in Islam. In contrast, people who accept whatever they experience and consider it as a part of a message God sends to them should praise God to show their faith. "Praise God" means that they accept what is taking place in their lives. Often, Muslims are misunderstood for their praise of God in such circumstances (El-Islam, 1982).

Prophet Mohammad related to God as a companion whom he could communicate with indirectly through Gabriel and directly through the mind and the emotions. He was constantly having monologues *Monajat,* that is, silent spiritual talks with God. Prophet Muhammad related to God as the ultimate love. People in distress relate to their experience as a chance to learn to become religious and spiritual and follow the way of Prophet Mohammad (*Sunnah*).

Trauma and Locus of Control

According to Kubler-Ross (1969), a person goes through five stages in the process of grief and remedy: denial, anger, bargaining, depression, and acceptance. When a Muslim shows an immediate acknowledgment of the loss and declares to accept it by declaring, "Praise God, I lost my daughter," this makes stage 5 the first stage. This act taken by grieving people represents total obedience to God. People around the mourning person will remind her or him to show total obedience to God by accepting "His judgment."

It seems that among Arab Muslims, grief is the perfect time to remind people regarding their relationship with God "the owner of all souls and spirits, who sends them as gifts and claims them back." If people decide at time of distress to show anger, Muslims believe that they may experience more loss. Therefore, people are trained and often are helped to show immediate acceptance of loss. Arab culture accepts and even praises persons who stay in depressed mood after a tragic loss or who emerge from the loss totally in religion and spirituality and abstain from all life comforts (Abu-Baker, 2004; Al-Krenawi & Graham, 2000).

In psychological terminology, Arabs use God as an external locus of control by internalizing the deep belief system that "everything in our life caused by God." This praxis affects the development of Arabs' sense of responsibility over their plans, lives, and work (Rashid, 1979; Weiner, 1974).

Frazer (1976) understands religiosity as fawning and seeking closeness with supreme power that is believed to direct the course of humanity and nature. In Frazer's view, religiosity is in part practical effort to please, satisfy, and come close.

When my husband became seriously sick, my mother was convinced that an evil eye caused harm to my life. She vowed a 170 cm long candle—as tall as I—to St. George who is also known to Jews as "Eliaho Hanaveh" and to Muslims and Druze as "Alkhader." People in distress, who ask God for help, show their humility by addressing prophets and shrines that belong to other monotheist religions (Badri, 2016). In exchange for his favor in asking him to keep me protected from evil eye, my mother bought a green satin cloth and covered the grave in the prophet's shrine as a gift.

During the same period, my husband's siblings organized a ceremony that is called "*Mauled*" that translates literary as "the birth." In this ceremony, a "*Sheikh*" recites the story of the conception, birth, upbringing, and life of Prophet Mohammad. At the end of the ceremony, all participants appealed to God and Prophet Mohammad, asking to cure the sick person. The ceremony has a spiritual component where people deeply believe that the soul of Prophet Mohammad will be present and listen to the prayers.

During that year, a relative who made the Pilgrimage to Mecca took my husband's shirt in order to pray on it and let it touch the *Qa'ba* and plead for his health.

Each of the above ceremonies was initiated when people knew that science could not help. Persons who were spiritual used religion as a tool to empathize with a person who experienced distress (Utz, 2011). These ceremonies can be organized and performed individually or by a group. When a group is invited, the ceremony has the effect of group therapy while the prayers and the chanting help in charging the atmosphere with spirituality. The ceremonies functioned as a way to declare that the case was severe, and that only a combination of the power of science and the power of spirituality could make change happen. Leading or participating in the ceremonies acted as an element of empowering for hopeless people and, paradoxically, prepared them for the next stage: the loss.

While writing this chapter, I experienced a sudden traumatic occasion. In the first minute, when I was encountered by the bad news, I found myself reciting "Praise God, Thanks God." In retrospect, I learned that during that minute, my mind was counting all the endless ways I could experience trauma, including loss of beloved ones or other kinds of serious damages in to well-being. This was another type of "comparing, bargaining, and concluding." During that speedy calculation, I had concluded that I would accept paying the price of this kind of traumatic event, regardless its harm, since it was still much easier to carry than all other scenarios I had imagined during that speedy minute. My conclusion is that the immediate silent acceptance of Muslims of bad news regarding their painful traumas is grounded in a deep religious and spiritual belief system. Their acceptance that is accompanied with their praise and thanks to God emerges from the bargaining process. In Kubler-Ross stage model, bargaining relates to the idea whether or not the event in question is reversible, while in Muslims' reaction, bargaining relates to a negotiation whereby accepting the current traumatic event has the result that God will save this person from other traumas or losses. I agree with Esposito (1988) and Kafaji (2011) that belief systems, including religion, influence the ways people experience their mental health.

Spirituality and Belief System: Visits from the World of "Afterlife"

Imam Al-Ghazali (1990) defines four components of the soul: *qalb* (heart), *roh* (spirit), *nafs* (self), and *aql* (intellect). They all compose a spiritual entity that governs and guides human thoughts and behaviors (Hasbullah, 2000). Muslims believe that the relationship between God and the human is very intensive. During sleep, God holds the person's soul. According to God's decision, the person gets up and proceeds with his or her life or not. It is written in the Quran:

> It is Allah who takes away the souls at the time of their death, and those who die not during their sleep. He keeps those (souls) for which He has ordained death and sends the rest for a term appointed. Verily, in this are signs for a people who think deeply. (http://www.noble-quran.com/translation/) (39: 42)

According to the Quran, a soul "*nafs*" keeps a person alive but a spirit "*roh*" is a supreme connection between God and the human being. When a person dies his spirit goes back to God; spirits never die (Mahmood, Sep 2005).

It is believed also that, when a person is very close to death, his or her sight will be transcendent and can see events that occur in other worlds. After hearing my sister on her deathbed, I experienced other close people talking about persons who came to them days or hours before their death and had promised to accompany them in their journey to "afterlife."

My late sister's son, who was 4 years old when his mother passed away, 1 week after her death, started suddenly to giggle joyfully and talk while gazing toward the empty wall. When he was asked to whom he was talking "to my mother, can't you see her?" he answered. He pointed to the place next to the wall where only he was able to see, listen, and develop an ordinary mother–son conversation.

My sister's spirit visited several times after that incident. The family learned that she was visiting during major events such as weddings, severe sickness, birth of a new baby, and so forth. She visited family members in their dreams. The person that saw her in the dream would describe it as a vivid vision with a salute to the person who had the special occasion. During the years, many family members had dreams of my sister. Whenever one had a dream of her, all would listen to the details of what she had to say. Those messages helped us believe that she was still a vibrant part of our family. My mother used to conclude "she came to visit us—she observes our lives, she knows all details about us—as if she is still with us." The last sentence summarizes the functionality of such "visits over dreams": it enabled a type of continuity of family and emotional tightness that calms down the pain of loss.

Adjusting New Learning to One's Own Faith

I attended the first course on transcendental meditation offered to Palestinians in Israel in 1987. I got my mantra, but since I did not understand the meaning of the word, could not feel connected to it. Therefore, I decided to use verses from the Quran instead. This brought me to a deeper insight into the meaning of the verses and uplifted me to a new level in my spirituality. Later in my professional life, I was trained in hypnosis, including self-hypnosis, which I mixed with my Islamic meditation. Throughout those sessions, I used to pose queries concerning ways I will be able to use Western theories in interventions respectful to Arab culture. Thinking about therapeutic interventions became a constant element in my spiritual meditation.

I worked as the only Palestinian Israeli family therapist and the only supervisor in my society for about a decade. When I needed a consultation regarding a case, I either contacted my Western family therapy friends who were culturally sensitive, or I meditated and got ideas that were helpful. I often start my meditation session by the saying "In the name of God" *bism Allah* and ask to send answers to my "alter mind." This process could be described as "self talk" that translates from Arabic as "talk to my spirit *Roh*."

Consultation with God

My request for consultation through my spirit is based on the idea of a special prayer that Prophet Mohammad initiated that is called "The prayer of consultation" and sometimes it is translated as "the guidance seeking prayer" *Salat Alistichara* (www.proz.com/kudoz/arabic).

The idea is that any person who confronts an important decision is able to pray this special prayer and pose a query for the decision in question. The opening of the special prayer starts with the sentences:

> Mighty God, I ask you to inspire me by your power and your knowledge and I ask for your incommensurable grace. Because you are able and I am not, and because you obtain the knowledge and I do not.

The special prayer ends with the sentence, "Let me accept the decision." The difference between my meditation and "the guidance seeking prayer" is that in meditation I am fully awake while in this special prayer a person should immediately go to sleep and wait for the inspiration that arrives in a dream.

The "guidance seeking prayer" is an example of spiritual communication with God through sleeping time—when spirit "*roh*" transcends during sleep time to reach the supreme connection with God. It is believed, that in that encounter, God attaches his message to the person's inquiry.

The last part in the prayer that asks for help in accepting God's message designates the nature of the relationship: The advice should be related to as a working plan rather than a suggestion. We conclude that when a person asks guidance from God through a spiritual path, he or she should decide beforehand that they fully rely on and accept all God's direction. In psychotherapy terminology, we may say "a person is ready to be in therapy."

The "guidance seeking prayer" *Salat Alistichara* functions consistently with constructionist theory; it allows to put one's self in a position of not knowing, looking up to learn and collect more knowledge, and be curious and ask to be taught what would be helpful.

Relying on God is the cornerstone of the external locus of control that characterizes most Arab Muslim people (Amer & Jalal, 2012; Yousef, 2000). People like Nuha, who were brought up to maintain both Western lifestyle that is reflected in dress code, education, profession, gender roles, individuation and Islamic lifestyle that is reflected in faith, worship, and the practice of rituals, are able to maintain a balance of internal and external locus of control. When Nuha surrendered herself to spiritual/religious therapy, she was promised by her ultrareligious sister that this would be an elevating spiritual experience that would help Nuha become closer to religion and to God. Western psychotherapy cannot offer this promise. When Nuha decided to start therapy with me, she felt already closer to God, protected from "evil soul," and could rely on her internal locus of control.

At graduate school, I became acquainted with Caplan's (1974) theory, "Support Systems and Community Mental Health." The theory advised scanning all "natural helpers" and including them in the therapy plan. Caplan related to clergy as "natural helpers." I questioned myself whether, as a future therapist, I would be able to find Muslim or Druze Sheikhs who would collaborate with me to help clients. I started studying Islam as a resource I would like to draw from it as a therapist. That was when I discovered the depth of the Quran as a psychological text and the common stories between it and the Bible regarding prophets and God messengers. This journey was another spiritual uplifting that helped my clients and me.

In my PhD program, as part of my research training, I chose to observe the social impact of Sunday mass in churches. I picked an Islanders church in Florida, USA, and made my participant observations for about 4 months. This project helped me plan and carry out my thesis research project on Arab families immigrated to the USA (Abu-Baker, 1997). I collected information in an Islamic center including participant observations, focus groups, and individual interviews for 18 months. In both places of worship, Christian and Muslim worshipers, who did not practice their religiosity in their original homeland before their immigration, felt proud to embrace their faith during those devoted hours, then to live their "American Western" life during the rest of the week. I drew common insights from the two projects: (a) the utility of religion and spirituality for reconstructing one's identity as an immigrant, (b) the psychosocial support of worship in a group that enhances spirituality and mental health, and (c) the circular relation between spirituality, social support, and mental health.

In conclusion, intersection of several factors influenced the developmental process of including spirituality within my professional life. (a) Religiosity and spirituality developed in my family of origin subsequent to a major trauma and loss. (b)

Political changes in the Middle East have accelerated the adaptation of Islam as an ideology and lifestyle for the majority of Muslims since the early eighties. (c) My training as a family therapist was influenced by the history of my family and by the resources influencing my professional and spiritual education.

In the next section, a few case examples will be introduced where spirituality and Islamic norms were used as helpful interventions.

Examples of Using Spirituality in Therapy

The state of Israel related to its Palestinian citizens as "the remnants of the enemy" and forced martial laws on them for 19 years. During those years, censorship intervened in the cultural and spiritual lives of Palestinians, trying to disconnect them from their heritage, including language, history, culture, and faith. More profoundly, they dehumanized each and every thing that belonged to Palestinians (Rabinowitz & Abu-Baker, 2005).

The development of the media in the Arab World helped spread the new socio-cultural and political phenomena of Islamization. The Islamic movement was established in the Arab world in the 1930s and spread out among Palestinians in Israel during the 1980s. Development of the Internet and satellites in the mid-1990s added to the variety of opportunities to renew Arabs', and among them Palestinians', faith and practice of Islam as a lifestyle.

In the field of psychology, Muslim practitioners from the Arab world began publishing their works about using Islam as a religious and spiritual resource in their clinical work (Ahmed, 1992; El-Islam, 1982; Okasha, Saad, Khalil, El Dawla, & Yehia, 1994; Rashid, 1979, Thorson, Powell, Abdel-Khalek, & Beshai, 1997). The umbrella of cross-cultural psychology and cultural sensitivity had legitimized this utilization of religious norms and spirituality in therapy.

Stories that are documented in the Quran are beneficial tools for bibliotherapy and narrative therapy for devoted and secular Muslims. In a case of cyber infidelity of a Muslim woman, the husband, according to Arab traditions, was eager to divorce her. The idea that her male relatives would kill her for causing harm to family reputation made him hesitate with his decision. The husband felt trapped in the nondecision situation. I discussed with him a similar story that happened to Prophet Mohammad, when people suspected that his beloved wife, Aisha, had a romantic relation with another man. I asked the husband to read about that story. The husband hesitated declaring that he was not practicing Islam in his daily life. I suggested that he read it as a story of another man who went through what he was going through with his wife. The next session, the husband said that he totally empathized with the psychological state Prophet Mohammad had experienced. My client was impressed with the way God had asked Mohammed, through a message he sent him as verses of the Quran through Gabriel, to learn that "some suspicion is sin," meaning, "do not misjudge" (The Quran, verse 49:12), when the suspected person would not be guilty. Being connected spiritually with Prophet Mohammad helped the husband to make up his mind and to work in therapy on the damage that was created in his marital life.

In another case, Ameer, a 46-year-old married Muslim man, who had four children, wanted to leave home and convince a married woman—whom he loved—to leave her husband and children and to live with him. He cheated on his wife all his life, including with her sister and her neighbor. Ameer never felt shame or remorse for his lifelong cheating. One session, I reflected my genuine feelings toward his life. I observed him as being "empty," without any social, religious, or spiritual norms. The following session, Ameer said that that was the first time ever in his life someone talked to him about spirituality. He had felt respected and equal to others when I questioned his spirituality. Later, learning more about spirituality, Ameer had discovered what he described as "a new life." Spirituality for him sounded human, open, nonformal, not dependent on strict acts of worship, rather on thinking, meditating, and relaxing. Ameer started reflecting deeply on his decisions in his life, and then made fundamental changes. His wife said, "You had used some magical words on him. He became a new person that session." From my observation, I did not judge Ameer's behavior, rather, joined him and was able to reflect what he was experiencing. That was a magical and spiritual moment for him.

Arabs and Muslims often feel pain from the gaze of outsiders, mainly, Israeli Jews and Westerners, who judge their spirituality as somehow "primitive." Should people describe Ameer as a person who went "backward" by adopting spirituality in his life? In Nuha's case, fear of this gaze was an element of keeping her religiosity as a secret from her social circle.

Conclusion

Spirituality is an outcome of personal and familial processes that are influenced and shaped by education, history, nationality, politics, class, and gender, and the intersectionality among them. Spirituality is a part of our psychic life and about who we are. Therapy and spirituality are extensions of each other. When psychology has the agenda of talk, spirituality can offer a tool for curing, guiding, and giving meaning for that same talk/experience. Therefore, discussing spirituality in therapy helps to understand clients in a deeper and wider way. Cases described in this chapter show that the combination of utilizing spirituality and using psychological knowledge made positive contribution to healing trauma. With that said, it is important to emphasize that for some people, it is easier, or feels more natural, to do spiritual work rather than psychological work. Both will lead to better well-being in a person's life.

Spirituality and psychology should consider the culture of the client. Sharing the process of the development of religiosity and spirituality in my family of origin helped me conclude that therapists learn from their own life experiences that deepen their understanding of human relations. Psychotherapy and spirituality carry the ability to change people and to relate to themselves and their culture in a new approach.

As a therapist, I often operate from within systems; I draw from a diverse pile of techniques, try to stay profoundly culturally aware, pay special attention to gender issues, and suggest my interventions from different faces of culturally sensitivity, and I combine spirituality and psychotherapy. I leave my post-modernism very loose to include new interventions. I describe my therapy work as "anthrotherapy." As an anthrotherapist, I respect clients' reliance on God as the cause of their problems and the source of its remedy. I abstain from diagnosing such clients as having external locus of control and refusing to take responsibility over their lives. Instead, I use elements from spirituality and religiosity to encourage clients to find ways to understand God's plans in their lives. Clients are encouraged to adopt proactive attitude in order to show God that they appreciate change he suggests in their lives.

References

Abu-Baker, K. (1997). *The impact of immigration on Arab families in South Florida.* (non published Ph. D dissertation). The Department of Family Therapy, The School of Social and Systemic Studies. Nova-Southeastern University. Fort Lauderdale, FL.

Abu-Baker, K. (Ed.). (2004). *Women, armed conflict and loss: The mental health of Palestinian women in the occupied territories.* Jerusalem: Women's Studies Centre.

Ahmed, R. A. (1992). Psychology in Arab countries. In U. P. Gielen, L. L. Adler, & N. A. Milgram (Eds.), *Psychology in international perspective. 50 years of the International Council of Psychologists* (pp. 127–150). Amsterdam: Swets & Zeitlinger.

Al-Ghazali, A-H. (1990). *On disciplining the soul.* (T.J. Winter, Translator). Cambridge: Islamic Texts Society.

Al-Krenawi, A., & Graham, J. R. (2000). Culturally competent social work practice with Arab clients in mental health settings. *Health and Social Work, 25*, 9–22.

Amer, M., & Jalal, B. (2012). Individual psychotherapy/counseling: Psychodynamic, cognitive/behavioral, and humanistic/experiential models. In S. Ahmed & M. Amer (Eds.), *Counseling muslims: Handbook of mental health issues and interventions* (pp. 87–118). New York: Routledge.

Arieli, A., & Aychen, S. (1994). Mental disease related to belief in being possessed by the "Zar" spirit. *Harefuah, 126*(11), 636–42, 692. (in Hebrew).

Badri, M. (2016). *Cultural and Islamic adaptation of psychology: A book of collected papers.* Manchester: Human Behaviour Academy LTD.

Caplan, G. (1974). *Support systems and community mental health: Lectures on concept development.* New York: Behavioral Publications.

El-Islam, M. F. (1982). Arabic cultural psychiatry. *Transcultural Psychiatric Research Review, 19*, 5–24.

Endrawes, G., O'Brien, L. & Wilkes, L. (2007). Egyptian families caring for a relative with mental illness. *International Journal of Mental Health Nursing, 16*, 431–440.

Esposito, J. L. (1988). *Islam: The straight path.* New York/Oxford: Oxford University Press.

Frazer, J. G. (1976). *The golden bough: A study in magic and religion.* London: The Macmillan Press.

Ghorbani, N., Watson, P. J., & Khan, Z. H. (2007). Theoretical, empirical and potential ideological dimensions of using western conceptualizations to measure Muslim religious commitment. *Journal of Muslim Mental Health, 2*, 113–131.

Hasbullah, M. (2000). Cultural presentation of the Muslim middle class in contemporary Indonesia. *Studia Islamika. Indonesian Journal for Islamic Studies, 7*(2), 1–58.

Hussain, F. A. (2011). *Therapy from the Qur'an and hadith: A reference guide for character development*. Riyadh: Darrussalam Publishers & Distributers.

Kafaji, T. (2011). *The psychology of the Arab: The influences that shape an Arab life*. Bloomington, IL: AuthorHouse.

Kübler-Ross, E. (1969). *On death and dying*. New York: Routledge.

Mahmood, M. (2005). Soul and spirit *(nafs waroh)* http://www.eltwhed.com/vb/showthread.php?2871-((%C7%E1%E4%DD%D3-%E6-%C7%E1%D1%E6%CD))-%E1%E1%CF%DF%CA%E6%D1-%E3%D5%D8%DD%EC-%E3%CD%E3%E6%CF. (Arabic).

Okasha, A., Saad, A., Khalil, A. H., El Dawla, A. S., & Yehia, N. (1994). Phenomenology of obsessive-compulsive disorder: A transcultural study. *Comprehensive Psychiatry, 35*(3), 191–197.

Peek, L. (2005). Becoming muslim: The development of a religious identity. *Social Religion, 66*(3), 215–242. https://doi.org/10.2307/4153097, Published: October 1, 2005.

Rabinowitz, D., & Abu-Baker, K. (2005). *Coffins on our shoulders: The experience of the Palestinian citizens of Israel*. LA: University of California Press.

Rashid, H. (1979). The message of specialists in mental health: An Islamic psychology. *Journal of Al-Muslim al-Muasir, 18*(5), 113–122. (Contemporary Moslem).

Sengers, G. (2003). *Women and demons: Cult healing in Islamic Egypt*. Boston: Brill, Leiden.

Shouby, E. (1951). The influence of the Arabic language on the psychology of the Arabs. *Middle East Journal, 3*(5), 284–302. http://www.jstor.org/stable/4322293.

The Qur'an. (2015). *M. A. S. Abdel Haleem* (Translator). Oxford: Oxford University Press. 1976.

Thorson, J. A., Powell, F. C., Abdel-Khalek, A. M., & Beshai, J. A. (1997). Constructions of religiosity and death anxiety in two cultures: The United States and Kuwait. *Journal of Psychology and Theology, 25*, 374–383.

Utz, A. (2011). *Psychology from the Islamic perspective*. Riyadh, Saudi Arabia: International Islamic Publishing House.

Weiner, B. (1974). *Achievement motivation and* attribution theory. Morristown, NJ: General Learning Press. (http://www.noblequran.com/translation/) (39: 42). (http://www.proz.com/kudoz/arabic_to_english/religion/483421-%D8%B5%D9%84%D8%A7%D8%A9_%D8%A7%D9%84%D8%A5%D8%B3%D8%AA%D8%AE%D8%A7%D8%B1%D8%A9.html).

Yousef, D. A. (2000). The Islamic work ethics as a mediator of the relationship between locus of control, role conflict and role ambiguity. A study in an Islamic country setting. *Journal of Managerial Psychology, 15*(4), 283–302. MCB University Press.

An Unknown, Unnamable Journey: Family Therapists in Complex Conversations as Muslim and Sikh Immigrants

Kiran Arora and Saliha Bava

> Understanding comes to fruition only in the response. Understanding and response are dialectically merged and mutually condition each other; one is impossible without the other.
> (Bakhtin, 1981, Discourses in Poetry and Discourses in the Novel).

In the summer of 2004, in a conversation with my mother when I, Saliha, was visiting with my family in India, after having lived in the United States of America for nine years, I concluded that though she and I share the values of compassion, kindness, and love toward others, they stem from different moralities—a religious morality governs my mother while I draw on a humanistic morality. There is a difference in sensibility, and experientially the distinction feels vast even though the end result of an interaction might be similar. I think the distinction is illustrative of how we each negotiate our relationship to religion. As did I in my way, in their own way my parents negotiated their relationship to the practice of religion throughout their life. Not so much about their belief in God, but in the practice of religion. Thus, intersectionality of our identities was not lost on me even at a young age. We were raised to be religious and secular. Have faith and to be inclusive. Believe in Islam and celebrate other religious identities (Bava, 2016).

The spiritual and political aspects of Sikhism have always been woven together for me, Kiran. My father's message to me was to *have no fear*, also known as the concept of *Nirbhau*. He embodied the Sikh principle never to cower to oppression,

Author contributed equally with all other contributors. Kiran Arora and Saliha Bava

K. Arora
Long Island University, Brooklyn, NY, USA
e-mail: kiran.arora@liu.edu

S. Bava (✉)
Marriage and Family Therapy Program, Mercy College, Dobbs Ferry, NY, USA

Houston Galveston Institute, Houston, TX, USA

Taos Institute, Chagrin Falls, OH, USA

D. Trimble (ed.), *Engaging with Spirituality in Family Therapy*, AFTA SpringerBriefs in Family Therapy, https://doi.org/10.1007/978-3-319-77410-7_3

but to stand up to it, confront it, and to defend others who may not be able to. My mother expressed the spiritual realm of Sikhism, emphasizing a focused intent on prayer to calm the mind. She firmly believed that having a disciplined practice of prayer would center and heal me. Sikhism is firmly rooted in the belief that everything happens according to God's will. The focus of the prayer was to have the strength to accept God's will in its entirety. My parents helped me internalize the Sikh concept of *Miri Piri*, or the *temporal and spiritual components* of life. These are the messages that were taught to me during my own moments of sadness and despair and help anchor my spiritual life.

In writing together, we have wrestled with questions such as, *how do we, people of marginalized religious faiths navigate the current cultural context in Northern America* and *how are our relational processes informing our therapeutic practices* and *in turn shaping our identities*? In this paper, as we converse about our journey of religious identity, we reflect on context, community, self, and mental health. We also reflect on how our identities are shaped by the intersecting discourses we navigate, and on sense making as an ongoing constitutive process of being responsive to self, other, and community. Further, we share with you practice implications derived from our personal, spiritual, and therapeutic reflections. We conclude with case examples that highlight these implications in teaching and clinical settings.

Our Faith Identities in Conversation: Our Process of Writing

This chapter is written alongside multiple conversations we have with one another. Through this journey, we have discovered, uncovered, challenged, and embraced our notions of religion and spirituality. New questions emerged as we continued to engage in the active processes of listening and understanding. As we shared our experiences, we found ourselves talking in terms of insider and outsider discourses of our faith communities. Insider discourses are stories of faith that we grew up with along with stories from other believers within the faith community. And outsider discourses are how people from outside of the faith speak about our respective faith; they can be media, people of other faith, and/or nonbelievers. We have questioned how to write without negotiating with the outside and inside discourses on our specific faiths. The reader will inevitably make meaning of our writing through dominant discourses on Islam and Sikhism, taken for granted ideas that have added to the landscape of meaning of these two faiths. As writers and practitioners of the faiths, we too have had to deconstruct and question these powerful discourses in an effort to get to the sense of our experiences. Our hope is to make adequate space for our realities, our stories, our interpretations, and to have them stand on their own without apology.

We write not only in first-person narrative but also to share what are marginalized faith narratives that are often obscured in the current context of creating homogenous narratives of faith communities. Our stories are not intended to be reflective, but rather constitutive. How might we ask you to be open to the performative quality of your reading by which our stories are performed and remade in your internal discourse? How might we be present to this as an isomorphic process both in the clinical and social realms?

Location of Self

I, Kiran, am a South Asian, Sikh, Canadian woman living in the United States. My relationship to my faith has been a mostly private affair and I have come to believe that God is not limited to my understanding and will be mostly unknowable through my lifetime. I am committed to the journey of deep reflection and transformation of self that requires an ongoing engagement with my spiritual life. My parents were born in India and migrated to Canada in the 1960s and 1970s. Their experiences with internal religious conflict and war in India, along with the country's poor human rights record, forced them to immigrate to Canada. Stronger economic and social opportunities were a pull in their migration. Despite Canada being a more stable democracy where religious freedoms and human rights are more likely to be respected, my family has not been free of discrimination due to race, religion, and gender. My own life has been marked with incidents of discrimination that I continue to comprehend and heal from. My migration to the United States follows my parents' legacy of pursuing a greater dream, greater stability, and healing from wounds that seem to be bound to time and location.

I, Saliha, locate myself in relationship to religion and spirituality, or for that matter to any other social identity, as having a hyperlinked identity (Bava, 2016). Such a dynamic identity is a contextually situated way of defining oneself in which we weave or link our stories of identities/becoming, which can be imagined as different fragmented texts. There are many different ways of creating these linkages and creating a multivocal construction of "who I am" (Bava, 2016). Just like surfing the Internet in search of a concept or meaning, with every click on a hyperlink we can gain greater clarity or get a bit confused, depending on how we make meaning. Similarly, the way we navigate from one linked story of ourselves to another, we create different stories about ourselves depending on the relationships and contexts we inhabit. Thus, one story of my relationship to religion is that I grew up in an Indian military family where religion, Islam, was foundational to our family life. Religion and culture, especially the cultures of Delhi and military life, were deeply intertwined. For instance, I experienced more liberation as a Muslim woman than as a Delhi girl. Or I experienced more constraints as a child being raised by a mother of three daughters whose husband (my father) was posted away from the family due to his military duty. However, it is hard to separate out these intricately intertwined threads. It guided our everyday practices and performances from eating, drinking, dressing, and conducting ourselves to relating to people. It has informed my humanistic stance and opened me up to complexity, diversity, and celebration of differences that I seek in life (as detailed in Bava, 2016).

Context and Religion

The intertwining of the political and spiritual has been a consistent theme in the history of Sikhs and continues to this day. From the inception of the faith, Sikh Gurus suffered religious persecution and much martyrdom. Sikhism arose as a direct challenge to the religious and political oppression unleashed by the rulers of the time. Punjab, a state in India and the birthplace of Sikhism, as a whole has witnessed much political and spiritual turbulence.

Sikhism rejects social inequality of any kind. Sikhs have a long history of critiquing inequity and political oppression. Uplifting and working for the underprivileged and being a change agent for the marginalization of women and those in different religions, castes, and abilities have historically been a practice for Sikhs. The value of social justice is deeply engrained in the Sikh psyche as well as the idea of nobility for each person.

The partition of India in 1947 split the province of Punjab between Pakistan and India. This time is known as the largest mass migration in human history (Cutts, 2000) and is a major marker in my (Kiran's) family's history. As a 4-year-old my father with his family migrated across the border into the new India, leaving behind their home and possessions. Thousands of Sikhs, Muslims, and Hindus were killed in retributive genocide between different faith groups. My father had a memory of his father carrying the Guru Granth Sahib (the central religious scripture and considered to be the final Guru following the ten living Gurus) over his head, as a sign of respect as he walked across the border. The essence of this story as my father had expressed to me is that when life presents you with unbearable hardships that you cannot comprehend, keep your Guru close, as the Guru will see you through. The trauma of war, migration, and resettlement was softened by the family's faith in the Guru.

Several political events that took place in Punjab touched my family. The Punjabi Subha movement in the 1960s aimed at creating a Punjabi-speaking majority state where the Sikh identity could be preserved. My father, grandfather, and other men in the family were jailed during this time for protesting the Indian government's resistance to creating a Punjabi-speaking state. The women were forced to stay in their homes and protect their children. Other events included a series of political events in the 1980s and 1990s in Punjab that led to the crackdown on Sikhs by the Indian military, followed by the gruesome 1984 genocide of Sikhs. Grave human rights violations took place against Sikhs for years and to date nobody has been prosecuted. My family in India has been directly affected by these violent acts that continue to impact our lives today. Many diaspora Sikh families have been deeply impacted by these incidents in very tangible ways. I grew up at a time when Sikhs were on the headlines of the national news on a daily basis. The tensions did not remain within the borders of India. Many Canadian Sikhs were allegedly tied to the uprising and resistance to the Indian government and the desire to create an independent homeland. This is the context that I grew up in, where religion, politics, and one's safety were inextricably tied together.

The partition of India by the British also left a legacy of Hindu–Muslim conflict in the Indian subcontinent. Today we see the rise of Hindu nationalism in India where there are roughly 172 million Muslims (14.6% of the Indian population) (2011 Census, n.d.) and thus making India the country with the third largest Muslim population in the world. Similarly to Kiran, as far as I, Saliha, can remember, religion has always had a political subtext for me, even though those would not be the words I would have used as a child. As an Indian Muslim girl growing up in a military family context, I was cautioned to be careful. My dad would let us know that since he was a Muslim in the Indian Army, there was a file on him because of the discordant relationship between India and Pakistan resulting in strife across the borders. I have a memory as a child in elementary school, when there was an aggression between India and Pakistan, I sensed tension at home because my dad was actively engaged in troop and supplies movement. He cautioned us to be careful of how we talked. Though I didn't understand at that time, looking back over the years and connecting the dots, I realized that he didn't want his absolute loyalty to India to ever be questioned based on his religious identity.

Another source of the political underpinning to my religious identity flows from my mother's bedtime stories about Islam. When my father was posted away from our family during his tenure in the Army, as a child I would sleep with my mother, while my two older sisters slept in the adjacent room. My mom would put me to sleep by telling me religious stories as a way of cultivating a sense of religiosity and understanding for Islam. However, as we know, what one hears doesn't always correspond to what the teller intends. I believe my mom's intention was to inculcate in me the moral base for our religion, but the types of stories that have stuck with me are the ones that seem to have political underpinning to them. For instance, I remember the story of Prophet's first wife, Khadija, who was a businesswoman and older than he. So, I took away the message it is ok to be a businesswoman. Another message was about education; should one have to travel from Arabia to China in search of education, one should do so. These messages emphasized the values of identity and conviction as a woman. And the clearest message that has stayed with me is that religion has to update itself with time. Since some of the local customs of the Prophet's time influenced the emergence of religion, we need to adopt the spirit of the message and practice as it applies in today's context. Whether intended or not, I also derived these messages from the stories I was being taught while learning to read the Quran in Arabic from a teacher.

As I reflect, it is not lost on me that my mother's father valued education for his oldest child, my mother, and she did her very best to live up to her father's last wishes by going on to earn her doctoral degree. And even though she was raised by a very devout Muslim woman, my maternal grandmother, steeped in religious healing traditions but with limited formal education and who wore the hijab all her life, my mother never took to the veil or covering of her head. Was this my mother's way of adapting to the current times? Also, I wonder how my mother's academic focus on political science shaped her relationship to religion. My mother is a very devout Muslim woman herself, but she taught me to understand the spirit and not only the ritualistic traditions of the religion.

Thus, not only am I sensitive to the political underpinnings of religion, these experiences also made me sensitive to the politics of religion. We see with increased terrorism in the name of Islam and discrimination in the name of terror management, that religion is but a tool for political gain in the macro landscape of nation-states. The partition of India and Pakistan was just one example of it. And it continues to date in Indian politics, in American politics, and the world politics. Even if I seek to escape, I cannot. Thus, religion for political gains often plays out in our personal lives. The politics of religion shapes personal identities. The political is personal and the personal is political. As I seek to preserve my sense of freedom in the contexts of ever increasing Islamophobia and fundamentalist interpretations of Islam, I increasingly see how the personal is political. I see the need to fight for my voice, my version, and my expression of religion (Bava, 2016). And the decision to write this chapter is a way to preserve my personal choice by political action to tell my story, my version, and my voice. It is my way to resist a hegemonic view of Islam in the face of politicizing of Islam—fundamentalism, terrorism, and/or Islamophobia.

Self, Community, and Faith

The relationship between self, community, and faith can be intricate. There are many benefits to being connected to our faith communities. Communities instill a sense of belonging. They provide modes of expression for faith and opportunities for reflection and learning. There have been times when we have raised our communities above our faiths, giving importance to the community story of how to live as faith-based and spiritual women, while choosing to internalize our own ideas and voices. Both of us have had to navigate this delicate terrain. We have both been engaged in finding ways to transcend our communities and certain messages within those communities so we are better aligned with our personal unique spiritual journeys. We choose to participate in our communities while challenging notions of religion that feel limiting or different from our lived experiences. For instance, I, Saliha, married a man who isn't a Muslim. Based on this action, one might question my faith; yet, this is a way to also question a religious practice where men can marry a woman who is not a Muslim, but women cannot. One explanation for this is because the child from such wedlock will follow the father's religion. This interpretive explanation is not only based in religion but also on the cultural traditions of the times when Islam was born. And there is no question that such an interpretation is patriarchal even though other interpretations are possible.

Communities can become agents of social control, and the policing of faith can become an obstruction to personal expressions of faith. We have continued to question the dominant discourses of our faiths often enforced by community while remaining engaged and participating in meaningful dialogue and relationships. I (Bava, 2016) believe that transcendent faith is achieved when "belief and faith based on critical dialogue transcends the collective dominant discourse in its performance and is illustrative of one's preferred narrative" (p. 2).

Religion and Clinical Practice

For myself, Kiran, I deeply hold a commitment to social justice. I continue to evolve and to understand my own biases. It has taken several years of focused work to incorporate the idea of justice in my own life. Because of this process, I have patience and a nuanced understanding of my clients' own evolution toward their understanding of their lives.

I am highly attuned to circumstances in which my clients are feeling unjust treatment or control. My own experiences of oppression and the long legacy of injustice experienced by members of my faith have me listening deeply for these stories. At the core of my work is the commitment that all persons feel emancipated from their struggles and from ideas that are constraining. My work centers on transformation and healing that in my earlier life were described to me by my spiritual tradition.

My experiences have taught me to be more curious, beyond the story that the client is telling me. They have taught me to be more patient in the unfolding of the narratives. Some of the stories that come forth are half-told, half understandings, and it takes time to come to a more complete understanding of the ways in which the world impacts us.

My family's capacity to witness, hold, and heal pain has left me with my own ability to do the same in the therapy room. With my own communities of support, I continue to bear witness to challenges and triumphs as well as create opportunities for transformation and connection.

I, Saliha, come from a tradition of healers in my family. My family stories include, both on my maternal and paternal sides, extended family members who were seen as healers in their local community. Family members would have a vision when sleeping and were called to minister to pregnant women in labor. Also, some of the healers followed in the Sufi tradition. I have often wondered if my chosen path is the modern-day version of my family's legacy. As psychology replaces religion in our search for answers, are we turning to therapists to have the kinds of conversations one would have had with their spiritual guide? Is this why we sometimes refer to the therapeutic space as a sacred space? Often, I feel that my best in therapy comes from what I call being lost in the conversation, not seeking to consciously make sense, rather being carried by it. And I often refer to it as "being in a trance." Or being guided by what is emerging and trusting how my questions will connect various threads within the conversation *with* the client. When I try to be clever, I fail. When I stay in the process of pure wonderment, or what Csikszentmihalyi (1990) calls flow, creative connections are often made. It is hard to put into words what I often feel are experientially different forms of me in these relational spaces. Is this a spiritual moment that Rivett and Street (2001) speak of? And what are the implications of speaking about therapy in this way? And what are the implications of not speaking in these words?

I, Saliha, view therapy as a relational space where we explore life's ambiguities and unknowns in conversation. I believe one thing that is certain is the constant change we experience in life. With change come uncertainty and a need to relate to it. Each of us cultivates practices to engage uncertainty. And religion may be viewed as one such practice to anchor us in the midst of life's uncertainties. In India, prayer is often recited at the initiation of any life event to evoke the blessing of Gods to guide one through the unknown forces. Everything from a new day to a new life or project is blessed with special prayers both in private and public spaces.

Religion, as a cultural tool of sense making, provides people with a unique resource for resilience, which can be explored in clinical practice (Walsh, 2009). For instance, a client might get tarot card readings and then come to therapy to discuss her sense of the readings. The tarot card readings might offer a doorway to making sense of her challenges and it can help us not only to listen and ask questions from within her way of sense making but also to honor her practices of anchoring herself in the midst of an uncertainty.

Keeping the Gates of the Soul Open

Given the hardships my, Kiran's, ancestors have experienced in preserving their faith, the current climate that I live in feels to be an extension of their struggle. This climate of fear and divisiveness, of paranoia and hatred, or being under attack because of the faith one practices or the way one looks bears resemblance to the climate my ancestors have survived through time (Arora, 2013).

There are times where I feel that I do not have the same level of grit that my ancestors had, that my parents possessed. The constant barrage of media rhetoric, of the racial, gender, and religious discrimination I experience both subtle and overt, has taken a toll. There are times where I want to shut down. My body and my relationships bear the scars of the impact of the social context we live in. Yet, the resiliency and the sweetness of my parents' life keep me from truly shutting down. I have watched them resist the forces that worked to take away their freedom to live in a country that is not their own. I have watched them stand up to job discrimination because of their brown skin. I have witnessed derogatory language being spewed at my father because of his turban. Yet my parents not only survived, but also thrived with dignity.

There were many reasons for them to shut down, give up, and lose faith. However, their unwavering faith in God and ability to move through hardship is a value that has been passed on to me. I believe that in any single moment I have the ability to reach deep into my spirit and expand beyond the hardship that is facing me. For me this expansion is nothing short of God's or a Spirit's work. It is beyond my immediate comprehension, yet I have faith in the realm that is outside of my understanding.

For me, Saliha, religion and its practice have always been private. I have often led with what I call my "hypertext identity" (Bava, 2016), which is situated and constitutive in interaction with others. And yet, I find that living in the United States for the last twenty years, I have continued to become more public with my views of practice as Islam has been politicized on the world stage. Quantitatively, my published scholarship leans more toward auto-ethnographically styled papers as a Muslim practitioner (rather than as a scholar of Islam) as compared to all of my other areas of scholarship. At every step as I experience religious strife, where Islam is questioned or there is rising Islamophobia, I feel like wishing it away. Yet, I come forth and write my way through it as a way to be agentic about expanding the public conversation while also not being personally silenced. This is my way to keep the gates of my soul open when I'm surrounded in fear and oppressive discourses. Call it a mindful practice for my relational, social, and mental health; a form of activism.

Practice Implications Derived from Our Personal, Spiritual, and Therapeutic Reflections

> The religious and scientific traditions simply construct the world in different ways. We have erred for centuries in pitting these traditions against each other, and in the same way we have mistakenly pitted materialism against spiritualism, voluntarism against determinism, subjectivism against objectivism, and a host of related and misleading binaries. The important questions, as I see it, are how these various discursive traditions function in our lives together. What do they bring to us; what do they suppress; who is benefited and in what way; who is harmed? (Gergen, 2016, p. 78)

Drawing on Gergen, the question for us is whose moral order will we privilege in therapy? Is therapy part of the scientific tradition or something bigger? Therapy is one of the spaces in our lives where we explore meaning of our experiences, relationships, beliefs, and life. And spirituality "is defined as referring to the human experience of discovering meaning, which may or may not include the concept of a personal God" (Rivett & Street, 2001, p. 460). Resisting the current cultural move to legitimize psychotherapy scientifically, we propose that we need to locate it within a larger discursive tradition of healing and wellness that predates Freud and dates back to various wisdom traditions including religious and spiritual practices. Thus, we adopt both "instrumental" and "metaphysical" approaches to spirituality and religion in our clinical practices (Rivett & Street, 2001).

Therapy, Like Religion, is Not Apolitical

Both the theories and the context within which we practice are shaped by discourses of health, relationships, and effectiveness. Religion is an epistemological position—a way of knowing. All epistemologies are political. And one of the things we have learned about the political nature of our living is, that we can make them Truths, if we don't hold them lightly and stay open to what else is emerging. Clients have their own ways of knowing. Thus, our job is to listen for our clients' epistemology and not be impositional with our own in the way we ask questions, but rather offer our alternative epistemology as a possibility. By attending to how we are listening *with* our client's logic, we strive to create space for different perspectives and avoid colonizing our client's or student's views, and instead help make the implicit more explicit.

Religion is Cultural

In our conversations, we both recognized cultural stories. Religion often becomes a vehicle for culture. And religion also varies across cultures. As mental health discourses openly embrace religious discourses, we have to continue to attend to what is also neglected. For instance, Sufism, Shamanism, and Voodoo are all forms of local spiritual practices that have been obscured by psychotherapy practices. And to engage in a culturally contextually relevant dialogue with our clients (Hines, 2016), we need to learn from and with them about their spiritual practices. For instance, Petry (2016) illustrates how spirituality can be explored over the life cycle as we unpack the cultural stories of anxiety, depression, poverty, oppression, interfaith marriages, and/or aging. Religion is both a carrier of culture and carried by culture. In training, as we explore self-of-the-therapist issues we need to attend to how students speak of their local practices, including being a nonbeliever. We remain curious.

Negotiating Realities

While curiosity is central, it is not enough. As hosts of conversations, we also have to attend to how we are relating (McNamee, 2004), both to each other and to the context that is recursively being created from within our relationship (Bava, 2017). Telling one's story of religiosity is no different from telling other stories or from how we negotiate our relationships. All relationships are negotiated realities. In negotiating these realities, we are constantly remaking our contexts, which in turn shape the relationship and the conversation. In the process of writing this paper, we discovered that the experience of negotiating one's religious identity felt different from negotiating other identities in other contexts. We discovered that within a context (of country or of relationship) where one's religion doesn't enjoy an equal status, we are negotiating from a one down position. Such a constant negotiation, from this one down place, made the process not only difficult but also created a potential context for being silenced and/or forcing the choice to fit in. It is a constant process of negotiating how to be "spontaneously responsive" (Shotter, 2006) into uncertainty, into the unknowable. Consequently, in therapeutic and/or learning context, the question that arises is how to coordinate (Gergen, 2016) and be responsive (Shotter, 2006) in conversations where faith and religion are central to the conversation? How do we not get silenced in the face of a larger cultural discourse that creates supremacy of certain religions over others? Even though we might be curious with our clients and students, we also have to be contextually present. We have to create space for the complexity of negotiating and coordinating the conversation of religion within the context of dominant beliefs and nonbeliefs represented by the interlopers and the dominant political context within which the conversation might be occurring.

Honoring People's Voice and Their Right to Choose How They Tell Their Story

Just as we are aware that we wish for our voices and versions of religious practice to be honored, so do clients and students. They wish for their own voices to be honored. Voice and value are interlinked. So in listening, we are not only listening to their values, but also creating space for their voice to be heard and for them to be seen by their way of being seen. Each of us has a right to speak to our relationship with faith and the framework that shapes our stories. To exercise our right to choose our frameworks, we have to resist them being chosen for us by cultural traditions or discourses embedded in the media. Often, when we personally tell our story, it bumps up against the stories in the media and the people who consume those stories, creating a context that is not spacious enough to tell our own story (Bava, 2016). In our personal experiences, we have found some listeners tend to draw our story into their own frame of reference, rather than staying curious and open to changing their own frame. This raises the question often asked by Narrative therapists, "Who has the story telling rights?"

We believe that it is crucial to resist this process of media and cultural definition, while preserving each individual's personal choice to tell their story about their relationship with religion and spirituality, in the way they want to talk about it. Thus, in clinical practice, we practice the stance of curiosity and not-knowing (Anderson, 1997) as a way of being in inquiry about the client's preferred narrative rather than assuming their faith narrative based on our own understanding of their religious identity. We are curious how their story line developed for them within the dominant cultural context. We listen with care for how they speak of their relationship to the larger cultural discourse and their family's story line, learning what other stories intersected in the "choice" the person makes about their faith and its practice.

Case Examples

These two case examples highlight practice implications derived from our personal, spiritual, and therapeutic reflections. While this paper focuses on religion, we believe that at any given time, people are engaged in multiple discourses, negotiating their various cultural selves such as gender, and class, alongside religion. Segregated thinking often results in contrived divisions, which is why we encourage both/and thinking (Hardy & Laszloffy, 2002). Taking a more complex, holistic, and interrelated approach to understanding one's relationship to religion inevitably requires one to be curious about other parts that make the person's identity. The two case examples presented here include a stance of curiosity and complexity as well as an embodiment of our practice implications across therapeutic and teaching environments.

I, Kiran, worked with Bani, a 32-year-old Sikh American woman living in New York City. She came to therapy to talk about her recent divorce and the impact it was having on her life and relationships. She complained of difficulty falling asleep and a general lack of interest in life. Bani was married for two years to a Sikh American man. Much of her marriage was rife with disagreements and a lack of emotional and physical intimacy. The principle of gender equity that Sikhism espoused was a source of disagreement between the couple when Bani referred to it while highlighting her choice to pursue male-dominated career opportunities. During her first session she shared the pain of having her marriage break down, including some level of antipathy from extended family members who thought she didn't work hard enough to secure her marriage. Bani seemed stuck on the stories that particular family members had of her marriage that seemed to question her future prospects. Many of these narratives focused on the taboo of divorce in the Indian culture. While this was problematic for Bani, she was more concerned with her understanding that while marriage is highly regarded in Sikhism, there is no concept of divorce in the Sikh tradition. She shared her love for Guru Nanak, the first Guru in Sikhism who is known for his stance on social justice. Bani struggled with her place in the faith given her divorce, although this was not immediately clear to her. In therapy, I worked with Bani to contextualize her pain within the larger sociocultural and religious context. We worked diligently to decentralize the story her family members had on what occurred in her marriage and continued to make room for her to name the challenges and agony she experienced.

What emerged was Bani's intense sadness at feeling disconnected from her faith, which in the past had been a source of comfort for her. Much of therapy including rewriting her relationship to her faith and addressing complexities which once felt like dichotomies to her. Could she belong to a faith that did not recognize divorce? Who gets to decide on whether she belongs to her faith community? How did the religion's emphasis on gender equality and justice apply to her unjust marriage? Over the course of our therapy, Bani began to attend a Sikh women's group where she could engage in dialogue with other community members struggling with these questions. Therapy provided a vehicle for Bani to create a more complex understanding of her divorce, to develop greater self-compassion and the voice to articulate a more nuanced and empowering relationship to Sikhism. During our last therapy session, I asked her what she thought Guru Nanak might say about her divorce? She responded, "He would say, I am so proud of you."

In the Master's program in Marriage and Family Therapy at Mercy College, I, Saliha, introduced a self-of-the-therapist exercise at the beginning of the internship year. As a way of creating a learning community (Anderson, 1999) and a reflective learning context, each student explores their own ethnicity and shares it with the class. They read about their respective ethnicities as described in McGoldrick, Giordano, and Preto (2005) and present reflections on the chapter in terms of their own ethnic experience. The assignment is designed to not only help students learn about ethnicity as a carrier of cultural discourses but also the variety of ways in which these ethnicity readings, as received knowledge, can apply and not apply to the families we might help. By critically reflecting on the readings about their own ethnicity based on their personal experiences, they bring a critical gaze both to received knowledge and to their own life. The students develop a critically curious stance toward expert knowledge and for listening to people's stories. The exercise also opens up space for students to be curious about each other's practices and to give voice to their curiosity by asking questions. The students also reflect on the reading and how it is intersectional or not.

At Mercy, we attract a number of immigrant students and students of color to the MFT program. Often religion is one of the most common intersectional social locations (in addition to gender and migration) that students reflect upon based on their family practices and the readings. One of the most engaged aspects of these presentations is how to view and engage in their local practices of Spiritualism, Voodoo, Shamanism, etc. as practiced within their family-of-origin and how to bridge it with psychotherapy. Usually, there is a degree of familiarity of the local spiritual practices as bystanders but an absence of its practice in their own life. Often I observe a shift in the presentation tone. I wonder aloud with my students about the tone, asking if the tone embodies skepticism, or hesitancy, or something else? One of the student-presenters stated she was unsure how to place her country of origin's spiritual practice within the practice of psychology and therapy. When prompted to unpack what she meant by psychology, she identified her lack of knowing on how to combine her spiritual practice with DSM diagnosis, and whether they were incompatible. At times I continue to engage in a reflective conversation, with their permission, about their personal spiritual practices and their relationship to religion/spirituality. At other times I draw on this as an opening to engage the concept of *both/and* and how we hold contradictions (see case in Bava, 2017), or share a case example of how I engaged a client's deep commitment to tarot card reading with therapy or I might share a reading about the value of religion/spirituality and reflect on the notion of psychological science as western science that we are exporting to the world at large, and the need to be critical, reflective practitioners who have to learn to have complex conversations rather than look for a singular answer. At other times, I might have the class see Nigerian novelist and TED speaker Chimamanda Adichie's (2009) video on the danger of single stories and have them reflect on single stories in their life that are indeed plural. I see all these ways as conversational prompts for the rich dialogue that ensues and continues throughout the semester, as students see clients, and make connections between the presentation, dialogues, their personal experiences, and clinical cases.

By the simple activity of being curious about their tone of presentation, I'm inviting them to be public about the internal dialogue rather than being factual about the spiritual practice. I learn with them how they dance with their complex relationship to the concepts of religion, intersectionality, therapy, science, etc., rather than emphasize the factual religious practice. I'm curious how they developed their own relationship to religion and what were the constraining and liberating familial and cultural stories that guided this relationship. My goal is not only to create a learning context where we listen with curiosity and care but also to be inclusive of diverse religious practices while helping students to develop a critical reflective gaze toward all practices—religious and clinical—without outright rejecting that which initially we don't understand. I encourage my students to seek understanding by exploring their traditions with their family and community elders and not shy away from it.

By opening up the conversation, other students become curious and also start making connections to their own life, for instance, talking to the dead, creating altars, etc. For instance, one of the students reflected,

> I learned so much about myself and what caught my attention was the fact that I am exposed to a religion that many simply don't understand… These conversations have been shaping me as a therapist because it is strengthening my self-awareness. I have been hiding who I am for a long time, in order to satisfy my family, friends, and the social world. Therefore, learning about my culture, experiencing different things in life and talking about them has made me feel confident about who I am and what I can bring in my work field. (Anonymous, personal communication, October 9, 2016)

I find this critically reflexive exercise to be a resonant way to create a learning condition about identity and self as sociocultural processes. Such expansive conversations create teaching/learning moments that are not binary. Rather, students learn how to have complex conversations that are respectful of both believers and nonbelievers of faith, religion, and God.

Conclusion

In this paper we have attempted to underscore the ongoing fluid nature of the relationship between self and religion. Our religious lives are impacted by the many discourses we are embedded in. This includes but is not limited to family, national, political, media, and cultural discourses at any given time across our lifespan. We work from this premise as professors and therapists. This process of writing has been one of exploration, discovery, and co-creation. The elements of this paper came forth through multiple conversations and questions, which we posed to one another and then reflected on. Through these conversations, we discussed several practice implications for therapists and educators to keep in mind. These practice implications are honoring clients' voices; therapy not being apolitical; religion being a dimension of culture, right to choose and tell one's story; and negotiation of realities. We believe that our reflections are true in this moment and time, and that we will continue to explore, discover, and make meaning of our relationship to religion and its impact on our lives.

References

2011 Census. (n.d.). *C-1 population by religious community*. Office of the Registrar General & Census Commissioner, India. Retrieved from http://www.censusindia.gov.in/2011census/C-01.html

Adichie, C. (2009). *Chimamanda Adichie: The danger of a single story* [Video file]. Retrieved from http://www.ted.com/talks/chimamanda_adichie_the_danger_of_a_single_story.html

Anderson, H. (1997). *Conversation, language, and possibilities: A postmodern approach to therapy*. New York: Basic Books.

Anderson, H. (1999). Collaborative learning communities. In S. McNamee & K. J. Gergen (Eds.), *Relational responsibility: Resources for sustainable dialogue* (pp. 65–70). Thousand Oaks, CA: Sage.

Arora, K. S. K. (2013). Reflections on the experiences of turbaned Sikh men in the aftermath of 9/11. *Journal for Social Action in Counseling and Psychology, 5*(1), 116–121.

Bakhtin, M. M. (1981). *The dialogic imagination: Four essays*. (M. Holquist, Ed., C. Emerson & M. Holquist, Trans.). [Kindle Edition]. Amazon.com

Bava, S. (2016). Making of a spiritual/religious hyperlinked identity. In D. Bidwell (Ed.), *Spirituality, social construction and social processes: Essays and reflections* (pp. 1–17). Chargin Falls, OH: Taos Institute Publication.

Bava, S. (2017). Creativity in couple and family therapy. In J. L . Lebow, A. L. Chambers, & D. Breunlin (Eds.), *Encyclopedia of couple and family therapy*. New York: Springer. Available at: https://link.springer.com/referenceworkentry/10.1007/978-3-319-15877-8_226-1.

Csikszentmihalyi, M. (1990). *Flow: The psychology of optimal experience*. New York: Harper & Row.

Cutts, M. (2000). *The state of the world's refugees 2000: Fifty years of humanitarian action*. Geneva: UNHCR.

Gergen, K. (2016). Constructing spirit, spiritualizing construction. In D. Bidwell (Ed.), *Spirituality, social construction and social processes: Essays and reflections* (pp. 68–86). Chargin Falls, OH: Taos Institute Publication.

Hardy, K. V., & Laszloffy, T. A. (2002). Couple therapy using a multicultural perspective. In A. S. Gurman & N. S. Jacobson (Eds.), *Clinical handbook of couple therapy* (3rd ed., pp. 569–593). New York: Guilford Press.

Hines, P. (2016). The life cycle of economically fragile families. In M. McGoldrick, N. G. Preto, & B. Carter (Eds.), *The expanded family life cycle: Individual, family and social perspectives* (pp. 99–117). Boston: Pearson.

McGoldrick, M., Giordano, J., & Preto, N. G. (2005). *Ethnicity and family therapy* (3rd ed.). New York: Guilford Press.

McNamee, S. (2004). Therapy as social construction. In T. Strong & D. Pare (Eds.), *Furthering talk: Advances in the discursive therapies* (pp. 253–270). New York: Kluwer Academic/Plenum Press.

Petry, S. (2016). Spirituality and the family life cycle. In M. McGoldrick, N. G. Preto, & B. Carter (Eds.), *The expanded family life cycle: Individual, family and social perspectives* (pp. 156–171). Boston: Pearson.

Rivett, M., & Street, E. (2001). Connections and themes of spirituality in family therapy. *Family Process, 40*, 459–467.

Shotter, J. (2006). Understanding process from within: An argument for 'withness'-thinking. *Organization Studies, 27*(4), 585–604. https://doi.org/10.1177/0170840606062105.

Walsh, F. (2009). *Spiritual resources in family therapy*. New York: Guilford Press.

The Gift That Keeps on Giving: Culturally Relevant Integration of Spirituality in Family Therapy With African American Families

Paulette Hines

> I'd like to honor some of the women [and men] of our [recent] past who we should adopt as shining examples to emulate and inspire us as we fight for our future. These black women [and men] can and should be role models for people of all colors and genders. They were not ensconced in the ivory tower of academia. They were not politicians. They were women [and men] from poor and working-class backgrounds who against the odds—and at risk of death— decided to step up, speak out, organize, and challenge the status quo and the government. They are too often glossed over or passed over completely when history is being taught."
>
> —Denise Oliver Velez

Beliefs may function either as anchors during a storm or promulgate hopelessness and helplessness. What does it mean to say that one is hopeful or hopeless? How do people keep their spirits intact in the face of adversity, especially when they have been repeatedly dehumanized and oppressed? What differentiates people who emerge "bruised but not broken" from seemingly intractable challenges from those whose hopelessness becomes pervasive? How can practitioners succeed in being agents of hope and healing, particularly when we find ourselves coaching clients to keep hope alive in the face of situations that are far outside our experience and often in a context that involves swimming against the tide?

Seldom do clients walk in and ask for help dealing with their hopelessness. Yet, very often, the greatest challenge in working with clients, particularly those who have suffered historical trauma and face unrelenting life challenges, is helping them to access and sustain hope. The good news is that if hopelessness is contagious, so is hopefulness.

There are three potential scenarios when hopelessness poses a major challenge: There are times when clients convey hopelessness and therapists feel hopeful. At

P. Hines (✉)
Department of Psychiatry, Rutgers Robert Wood Johnson Medical School, Rutgers University Behavioral Health Care (Emerita), Piscataway, NJ, USA

D. Trimble (ed.), *Engaging with Spirituality in Family Therapy*, AFTA SpringerBriefs in Family Therapy, https://doi.org/10.1007/978-3-319-77410-7_4

other times, therapists feel overwhelmed and hopeless but the clients are either hopeful that their problem(s) can be resolved or are able to accept their adverse situation and stay motivated to pursue their dreams and find joy in life. I marvel at how some clients demonstrate exceptional wisdom and motivation to navigate their way to well-being while they contend with adversities that I can't imagine living through. A third scenario, and perhaps the most challenging, is when therapists and clients struggle with hopelessness.

In this chapter, I offer reflections regarding (1) my personal spiritual journey; (2) the interconnectedness of hope, spirituality, religion, and culture for me and other African Americans; and (3) the use of culturally congruent strategies and resources to address the ever-present issue of the hope and hopelessness that African American and other historically oppressed populations, as well as those who seek to serve them in the clinical, community, and larger systems arenas, confront on a daily basis.

Locating Myself

I am a heterosexual, educated, middle-class, married, semiretired woman of African American and Native American descent, mother of two sons, recent and proud grandmother. My fascination with the topic of hope and hopelessness began during childhood. I was blessed to grow up during the Civil Rights era in a small southern town, part of what some refer to as the "Bible Belt." In many ways, it was a living laboratory for the longitudinal study of faith, resilience, and resistance in action juxtaposed against the sobering reality that some succumbed to the challenges of maintaining psychological well-being in the face of unrelenting, systematic oppression.

My nuclear family (mom, dad, and two brothers) was part of an extensive extended family, the majority of whom lived within a twenty-mile radius including the four aunts and uncles who essentially functioned as my "second moms and dads." My family and community shared common values, for example, honesty, family, love, mutual respect, forgiveness, compassion for the sick and needy, hard work, education, striving to be one's best, gratitude, finding joy in life. They embraced the concept: "It takes a village to raise a child." Neighborhoods were racially divided, but economically diverse; middle- and working-class families lived alongside and supported each other.

Spirituality and religion were embedded in every aspect of our lives. Family, church, and community reinforced the Christian beliefs and values we were taught from the time we were able to talk. We were taught always to acknowledge God in our lives. I embraced the teaching about a higher power, went to Sunday School and Church weekly, giggled (a few times uncontrollably) at the "old folk" who cried and "testified" about how God had moved mountains in their lives, prayed before meals and going to bed at night, belonged to church organizations, attended church camp and vacation bible school. I enjoyed the privileges and challenges associated with the fact that my paternal grandfather, several paternal uncles, and, subsequently, cousins were well-known ministers in the region.

During my childhood, segregation was legal. I had an upfront and personal education about how religion can be misused to justify the oppression of others and to address the relevant question of whether messengers are acting on God's word or distorting the will of the Divine for their own purpose. I have candid memories of not being allowed to drink from the water fountains, use public restrooms, enter the front door of restaurants, or use the public swimming pool. I also remember acts of defiance such as giving back a cone of ice cream because I was told I couldn't sit at the store counter that was designed for that purpose. By the time I entered my segregated middle school, the Civil Rights Movement was in full bloom. While I had always been surrounded by people who engaged in acts of resistance, the demand for freedom rang in the air. I understood and shared the belief that there are some things worth fighting for, and embraced the cry that dignity and justice are worth dying for. Organized religion and activism were practically synonymous in my small world. Religious leaders and church members were highly involved in orchestrating and implementing efforts to promote social justice and change the racist practices that were supported by the laws of the country.

As a young teen, I drove my aging grandfather to church when his vision deterred him from driving. I sat through many of his sermons in awe of his potential to "move" his audience to their feet. I pondered the teaching that "God has a plan for each of our lives." I had been the beneficiary of people who understood the value of helping me feel loved, safe, competent, important, and prepared for life's blessings and battles. I questioned what purpose I would find in life but not so quietly hoped that I would not be called to follow in my grandfather's footsteps.

As much as I aspired to carve my own path, I have clearly chosen to follow in the footsteps of my ancestors. In the tradition of those who came before me, I consider myself a spiritual person. I believe in a divine force, known by many names, whom I call God. I do not think about or image God as having a shape, form, gender, or race. I have a sense of connection to all things in the universe, a great sense of awe for the order, simplicity, complexity, beauty, and interconnection between all that the divine has created.

As an adult, I opted and continue to belong to a church that espouses faith in action and is responsive to the social, economic, housing, education, and health needs of the surrounding community as well as our members. I draw strength and peace that defy words from the rituals, music, prayers, praise, and sermons that are designed to promote hope, survival, resistance in the here and now, and commitment to living life with concern and respect for others.

I resonate with Lockspeiser's (this volume, Chap. 7) reference to the construct of "ways of knowing." I share her belief that we can hear God's voice by listening with our hearts, being still, going into sacred space, witnessing the small and large wonders of the world (Walsh, 2009). I confess to being a product of my professional training. I own my ambivalence about sharing my truth...a revelation which no doubt speaks to the hesitancy our clients bring to their encounters with therapists. Is it ok to talk about this or that in this space with this person? This chapter is about acknowledging spirituality—clearing the path. Part of the rallying cry of social activists during my youth (and connecting the dots, my grandfather's signature promise each and every sermon) were the words…the truth shall set us free. Trusting this promise, my conversations with God have led me to confront *the truth* that God gives gifts to each of us. How we discover those gifts is always a subject of interest for me. Maybe the child jazz piano prodigy who (with no musical training) sat down at the piano for the first time and played superbly had a way of knowing upfront that defies all understanding? Nevertheless, we can choose or not choose to embrace our gifts from the Divine. I had an awareness as a child and, certainly as a therapist, that we bear witness to how far too many are robbed of their gifts as they go through life's journey. My gift (shared by many, if not all) might be easily named if I had lived within the tribal context of my ancestors, generations ago. I am learning to let go of the struggle to understand with my head and to embrace what I can only language as gut instincts, intuition, answers that come early in the morning accompanied with a sense of clarity and peace, and even the dreams that reveal what invariably comes true within several days.

I concede that my personal influences my professional! A well-known cliché is "everything that we need to know, I learned in kindergarten." Whenever I feel stuck in professional endeavors or personal life, I generally reconnect with another message my grandfather repeated often during my childhood: *Never say you can't.* This impressed me as his simple translation of biblical scripture, "I can do all things through Christ who strengthens me" (Philippians 4:13) ... a message of empowerment. It was not an invitation to be either grandiose or passive. It was his prayer that when we lack any clue about how to proceed, when we run out of steam and can't try, when we can't conceive what to do next, we exercise faith in God's strength and power. It was a message never to give up…dawn will follow night and after each storm, the sun will eventually shine again.

Connecting with the Past in Order to Move Forward

Struggle characterizes African American history, our present, and no doubt our future. African Americans have historically recognized that maintaining the will to live life to its fullest and never to give up is vital to our physical, psychological, and spiritual survival, and we have proved to be masters at doing so under unimaginable circumstances. Without hope, for example, the slaves who traveled the Underground Railroad would have succumbed, and the outward symbols of racist segregation would not have been outlawed. As we confront the challenges of the twenty-first century, the issue of "keeping our hope alive" remains central to the well-being and survival of African Americans. For the majority of African Americans, freedom from the shackles of slavery has not given rise to what some mislabeled a "post racism era," the morning after the Obama presidential election.

African and African American tradition involves looking to our elders for the wisdom they have drawn from their life experience. Yet connecting with the oppression that our forebears experienced both during slavery and since the Civil War era brings forth conflicting wishes for many African Americans: the wish to forget the inhumanity our ancestors suffered, and the wish to remember their amazing capacity not only to survive but to transcend difficult circumstances and overwhelming odds.

Countless recognized and unsung heroes and "s/heroes" were first physically enslaved and then segregated; the real victory was their audacity to believe in themselves, and to maintain a sense of dignity, self-respect, concern for one another, and hope for a better day. These were individuals who kept their spirits intact even though they were repeatedly treated as if they were dangerous or invisible. They had to struggle mightily to overcome the oppressive forces of poverty and racism.

In short, the African American story is one of unrelenting struggle—people searching for a way to be happy, to function at their fullest potential, and to be free from the scars of the past and the restrictions of the present. Lerone Bennett (1991) wrote "If we intend to redeem the pledges of the Black spirit, we must enter into an active dialogue with the voices of our tradition, which speak to us with recurring themes (p. 122)." Bennett suggests that the voices of the past speak to us of hope, endurance, and daring. They tell us that life does not exist in the absence of connection with family and our culture. They tell us, among other things, that nothing can destroy us *here, if* we keep the faith of our fathers and mothers and put our hands to the plow and hold on. They suggest that we can call upon the story of the collective and draw strength and direction.

African American culture is distinctive in the reliance placed upon oral communication to transmit beliefs, values, and traditions across generations. Proverbs and jokes, religious sermons and prayers, poetry, spirituals, the blues and other forms of music, and stories and fables drawn from African and African American tradition are rich in wisdom about endurance and remaining spiritually healthy in spite of unrelenting oppression. The premises contained within these vehicles may be linked to either secular or religious sources. They are highly intertwined and reflect the strong spiritual orientation that permeates African American culture.

Beliefs

There is a clear relationship between our beliefs and our social, emotional, and behavioral functioning. Hope is about more than optimism. It is about *believing* that taking action ("pressing forward" or "putting one foot in front of the other to accomplish something") is worthwhile. Weingarten (2007) thinks of hope as a verb, not just a noun; it is something one can do even when one doesn't feel it. As Freire (1994) argued, hope is necessary but not enough. To transform our lives, concrete action is needed. McGoldrick and Hines (2007) suggest that hope is not something we can give to others. "The mission of hope is to heal the wounds inflicted by all the ills of one's life. The importance of hope is that it prompts us to become the authors of our own lives." In accord, hope is a concept that is as central to spirituality/religion and therapy as it is to all life.

Spirituality and Religion

Elliott Griffith and Griffith (2002) define spirituality as "that which connects one to all there is." It pertains to a sense of harmony, connection between all living things and the universe. It may involve a belief in a divine spirit or an ultimate human condition toward which we strive. In a 2016 Gallup poll, nine out of ten (89%) Americans said that they believe in God or a higher power (Newport, 2016). However, one can be spiritual without embracing organized religion.

Certainly, spirituality, religion, and African American culture are so intertwined, many African Americans tend to hold biblically based beliefs. Cooper-Lewter and Mitchell (1991) have outlined a number of basic beliefs in African American culture that are tied to Judeo-Christian tradition and traditional African religion. These include reminders of the power of God (e.g., "God is in charge," "God knows everything and is an all-wise protector") and of the security that a just God offers (e.g., "God is just, fair, and impartial," "God is gracious, offering unqualified love," "God regards all persons as equal"). Common religious beliefs also pertain to the sanctity of life and basic human rights (e.g., "Each person is absolutely unique and worthy of respect"; "We should not surrender to the pressures of life and give up in despair"; "We are all related as a family."). The values that are encouraged by these beliefs parallel those espoused in the therapeutic community: forgiveness of self and others, self-discipline, respect for self and others, courage, honesty, ability to let go of negative emotional states, a sense of security, and so forth (Bergin, 1991).

When African Americans call upon religion-based sources of inspiration, we call not only upon the wisdom of our ancestors, but upon the power of a higher spirit as well. Family stories, fables, poetic prayers, daily meditations, sermons, and such hymns and spirituals as "Let Me Tell You How to Move a Mountain" and "God Can Do Anything but Fail" contain messages that encourage an outlook that we "can" bring to situations in order to triumph over obstacles. They proclaim that no matter how bad things seem, everyone's life is worth living. They encourage perseverance, forgiveness, not wasting one's time on vengeance, celebrating one's uniqueness, self-understanding, and unconditional love. They encourage us never to feel alone. They remind us that God is mighty; when God is our partner, nothing can penetrate our armor. Although we may not know what the future holds, we need not be fearful, for we know that God holds the future. They remind us that no one can take our joy in life from us unless we give it away. We can move from obstacles to possibilities. We can run a race with one foot, if necessary.

This narrative has particular appeal, given the adversarial context in which African Americans have lived in this country and far-reaching implications. In a conference presentation focused on the power of religious beliefs, the Reverend Buster Soaries (1994) (my spiritual leader) shared the following perspective:

> How do we account for the continued existence of African Americans in this country? For even when we were confronted by a political prison, when Blacks were in slavery and were not allowed to even meet together on a plantation, when we had to walk from Mississippi to Chicago— running from the Ku Klux Klan, when we were not even allowed to learn how

to read, when we fought in armies and then were not allowed to be buried in [military] cemeteries, when we had to walk past beautiful schools to go to one room school houses, when we had to live in houses with outdoor bathrooms and people down the street had beautiful mansions, we could still say we have access to the God of heaven and earth. And that sense of resolution gives us on the one hand the capacity to accept our conditions without giving in to our conditions—to live in the world but not be of the world, to hear the cries of the world but not succumb to the pressures of the world.

Folk Wisdom

The language and practice of hope, spirituality, and religion are intricately linked to culture. Among African Americans, interest in preserving the wisdom of our elders is apparent in the popularity of what are known as "books of affirmation" (e.g., Copage, 2005; Riley, 1993; Vanzant, 1993). These collections of old sayings, quotations, and proverbs drawn from African and African American experience are intended to pass on messages of empowerment. The messages that are conveyed have particular significance and familiarity for many African Americans. Some, such as "Stand tall, walk proud," and "Even an ant may harm an elephant," prompt us to let go of hopelessness and believe in ourselves. Others, such as "What storm is there which has no end?" and "Tough times don't last, tough people do," remind us that troubled times will come to an end. Yet others prompt us to take risks and to persevere: "If there is no struggle, there is no progress," "When life knocks you down, land on your back because if you can look up, you can get up," "You don't get there because, you get there in spite of."

Some proverbs connect us with our past and future, eliciting images of what has been and images of what can be. They draw attention to out interrelationship with one another through our commonalities in experience. Consider the power of messages such as "Our successes have been earned while we stood on the shoulders of those who came before us," "Reach back, give back," "Look from whence you have come," "You are the son/daughter of kings and queens," "Lose not courage, lose not faith, go forward" to energize, mobilize, and promote transformation. Their potential to tap hope defies simple explanation, both inside and outside the therapeutic process.

Inspiring Hope in Clinical Practice

We cannot give others hope, but we can help clients connect with hope's well-springs! That is to say, we can help them connect/reconnect them with the values, strengths, talents, and resources that can support them in their life journey. We can help inspire people to do hope by reminding them they are part of something larger than themselves and helping them to see themselves in multiple contexts (McGoldrick & Hines, 2007). They can summon the wisdom and spirits of their ancestors. They can turn to the tried and proven solutions passed down in their culture and families. They can reach inside to connect to that which has served as anchors: the Divine, their ancestors, each other, and those who will follow them in the future. They can be inspired to reach for a better day, despite real obstacles!

Regardless of whether their belief systems are grounded in secular and/or religious folkways, people vary in their abilities to readily articulate their basic beliefs. We are at risk, at any given moment, to experiencing a gap between our beliefs and values and what we do.

Therapists can help clients to pinpoint the basic beliefs that shape their worldviews, feelings, and behaviors by tracking their communications and asking direct questions. It is important to explore the personal meanings that underlie abstract statements (e.g., "I believe God will make a way") even when clients use a language that is familiar. The belief, in this instance, can inspire hope. But one has a choice about how to translate this belief into action. My aim in such instances is to help clients examine their perspectives and make their own conclusions about which beliefs and personal meanings they can let go because they are not serving them well.

I refer to one of the strategies I frequently employ with my clients as "*Stories of Faith, Hope & Resistance*." I aim to assume what Madsen (2014) calls an "anthropological stance" or genuine interest in learning from families about who they are, what they believe, what they stand for, their dreams, challenges, and attempts to get "unstuck." I listen for strengths, family/cultural legacies that have inspired them in the past, areas of demonstrated/potential vulnerability, resources they turn to "stay strong" and resist hopelessness, and any attempted "solutions" that ultimately sabotage their well-being and success.

Questions that I have found helpful to ask clients include

- What happened to you? How does what happened to you affect you now? How, in spite of what happened, have you been able to triumph? What external factors have contributed to your wounding? What needs to be healed? What gifts have you been able to bring forth from this wounding experience? What lessons/wisdom can you share with others based on your experiences? What would life in full power look and feel like to you (Jackson, 2012; Akinyele, 2008).
- What keeps you going in spite of ongoing adversity?
- Do you have a mission or calling, something that you think you are meant to do?
- Are there sayings or stories passed down to you that have special meaning for you when you face challenges? How might you operationalize this resource in your life now?
- What wisdom would your ancestors pass on to you if they could consult with us regarding your current concerns?
- What rules do you believe are important for you and your family to follow in life?
- What must you do to avoid giving up your power and dreams?
- How is the choice you have made consistent with the principles you embrace?
- What behavior would reflect caring for yourself and the people you love?

- What images or words from the past do you need to call upon to help you accomplish this difficult but very worthwhile goal?
- What were the beliefs you were taught when you were growing up that were meant to give you hope? What is your relationship to those beliefs now?
- What were the messages of hope that have enabled people of your culture to live beyond failure or pain?
- What have been the greatest adversities you have encountered in life and how did you push past them?
- Is there someone you especially admire in terms of their overcoming adversity and conveying a hopeful perspective?
- What messages about hope do you want leave for your grandchildren and others who will come after us?

Family discussions about the values, principles, and logic that undergird past and pending decisions about how to manage major life challenges can foster emotional shifts that are prerequisites for behavioral change. Such discussions provide me the opportunity to assume a non-pathologizing stance and to convey positive regard in cases where misguided decisions were driven by positive intentions (Hardy & Laszloffy, 2008). Helping families, especially those who face seeming intractable barriers, distinguish the factors in their predicament that are influenced by external forces and those which are self-imposed often prove to be of huge benefit. In doing so, I can *both* acknowledge the very real barriers that impede their well-being and movement toward their dreams *and* help family members take responsibility, individually and collectively, for addressing the gap between what they see themselves as standing for and their external behavior. Pinderhughes (1989) labeled the very real potential for one to unwittingly collude in one's own oppression as "victim responses to oppression." Connecting clients with their own familial/cultural legacies through the exploration of familial and cultural stories of Faith, Hope, and Resistance inspires clients to discontinue any behavior that reinforces their own powerlessness.

Hugo Kamya (Chap. 5, this volume) presents a poignant illustration about helping clients identify empowering metaphors. Referencing the goals of therapy, indeed of their lives, in language that rings truth in their hearts can be powerful. I find it helpful to introduce the metaphor of *pulling tools from a hope toolbox to feed the soul/spirit.* I prime/expand the client's engagement around the topic of hope by introducing brief examples of culturally congruent, "hope resources." These are selected excerpts from movies, songs, proverbs, videos, and documentaries that we view, listen to, read, recite, discuss during our session.

After clients unfold their Hope, Faith, and Resistance story, I subsequently engage them in a conversation about what practice (s) (e.g., prayer, meditation, art, writing, giving to others) and resource(s) (e.g., picture, song, poem, image, proverb) they turn to when they feel down and need to connect with hope and a sense of power to press on. If clients rely upon any concrete resources that they can bring in and share during our next session, I ask them to do so. I ask clients to begin assembling a variety of hope resources and to develop and implement a plan to use the tools in their personalized toolkit of hope to stay connected with the power of hope.

Alyson

In keeping with the space confines and focus of this chapter, I offer a partial case overview with representative examples of how I incorporate a client's hope, spirituality, and culture into "mini-" interventions that have impressed me as pivotal to positive client outcomes.

Alyson was a 58-year-old African American woman, previously married but divorced since young adulthood. At the time she first sought help, she was living on disability income. While she presented her grief over the recent death of her male partner of several years as the primary reason for her reaching out for help, it rapidly became clear that she was wrestling with a variety of interrelated, longer-term issues. She shared a history of repeated involvements in abusive relationships that she tolerated because she didn't feel worthy. She confided that she was drinking too much. Though she could not use the words at the time, she essentially shared her conclusion, framed as a question, that she was an adult survivor of childhood incest. She had long been preoccupied with the thought that something "not right" had happened to her as a child. She both adored her father and struggled to understand why he or anyone would hurt a child. She confided her belief that she was "bad," simultaneously slapping herself and digging her fingernails into her skin. She showed me carvings on her arms and legs that she had made with a knife that she kept at home for this purpose.

Alyson was perplexed that she was very exhausted most of the time and had begun to lie in bed for days at a time. She was forgetful, easily distracted, and had arrived at a point that she found herself unable to work. She experienced flashbacks in and out of session and described/exhibited dissociative responses (e.g., head jerking, child-like crying and speech, and referencing herself by her childhood nickname in the present tense), constant fidgeting, foot wiggling, and facial grimacing. She complained about feeling pressure in her chest, difficulty breathing, and a vague pain in her side.

Alyson acknowledged that she had purchased and periodically played with toy-sized tea sets. She acknowledged her awareness that neither this nor her habit of bringing two stuffed animals with her to therapy in a heavy bag was age appropriate or healthy. (We arrived at the conclusion that the bag was representative of all the confusion and chaos that existed in her life.). She complained that she was losing weight because she was not eating properly. She was inattentive as well to essential tasks like paying her bills and throwing out expired foods, and was basically socially isolated. By the time she came to see me, she had two former psychiatric hospitalizations. In her words, "I've given up so much of my life. I have been 'reaching for insanity to find sanity.'"

Alyson was the oldest of three children. Her siblings lived in different states. Both parents were deceased. Her father, a train conductor, had died from a stroke 10 years prior to contact and her mother, a practical nurse for a few years, had died 2 years after her ex-husband from throat cancer. She described both parents as heavy drinkers, especially on weekends. Alyson had grown up in the Midwest where there were few African Americans; she always felt “different” and had few friends. She and her siblings had vague memories of occasionally connecting with their maternal grandparents and extended family that lived in Georgia. She recalled fond memories of both and recounted a family story about her grandmother’s courage standing up to a neighboring man known to belong to the Ku Klux Klan. Unaware that her grandmother could read, the man had tried to trick her and her grandfather into giving up several acres of land but did not succeed. Her father’s single brother, who lived nearby, visited from time to time. He was a blues singer who died when Alyson was in elementary school. She described her parents’ relationship as highly conflicted. Alyson described herself as an over-functioning, parental child. Mom, described as “beautiful,” essentially took “leaves of absence” weeks at a time from the family. Neither parent ever offered an explanation about her mother’s absence.

Alyson distanced from her rage that her mother was not home and that she took care of her mom’s babies. Alyson’s parents formally separated during her teen years. She and her siblings initially remained with their father but went to live with their mother after he remarried. In recent years, she had written several poems acknowledging her dance between anger and empathy for her mother who died with unfulfilled dreams.

When asked about models for resistance, she evoked an image of her mom asserting herself with her head high when a white saleslady refused to acknowledge her and loudly used a racial epithet in response with Alyson and her siblings looking on as un-empowered witnesses. She spoke about her admiration of her maternal grandmother’s unwavering faith and her ability to make Alyson and each of her grandkids feel special. She also noted that Nelson Mandela was a favorite.

After leaving her home, Alyson had floated through college and adulthood with no sense of purpose, real connection, or power. The childhood abuse she “knew” she suffered represented a violation of trust, boundaries, and morality that left her spirit wounded. One metaphor that emerged from our dialogue involved Alyson being out in the ocean with no light—alone, swimming against the tide, struggling to stay afloat—a challenge that took all of her emotional and physical energy. The second was that Alyson had invested so much psychic and physical energy in distancing from her “truth” that she became a spectator …watching life from the sidelines rather than living it.

The work with Alyson evolved from multiple intersecting therapeutic goals and involved multiple strategies. Space prohibits a full description of the treatment process, but I do offer here examples of the “*mini-interventions*” and culturally congruent tools that were introduced to support Alyson in “doing” hope and some of the related outcomes.

Immediate objectives included affirming the courage involved in pursuing Alyson’s belief that she had endured sexual trauma at the hands of her father during her childhood; supporting her in revealing her "secret" to her siblings; heightening their understanding about trauma and its residuals; and inspiring Alyson to be *caring* towards herself, to believe that better days lie ahead, and to commit to a safety plan.

Guided by the premise that heightening her *connectedness* to her family, cultural, and spiritual roots was key, I followed Alyson’s lead and encouraged her to explore her grandmother's legacy, a topic that she had given no conscious attention. We subsequently viewed several segments of a documentary (Standing on My Sisters' Shoulders) about the ways that ordinary, courageous African American women created small waves that changed the landscape of America. I asked Alyson to view the full documentary before the next session and to consider in what ways she was committed to making her own small waves. She acknowledged "knowing" that she needs to find a way to use her ability to show caring for others and brighten their day. On another occasion, I asked her to watch the movie, *The Help*, and reflect on what she learned from watching. She was impressed by the courage of the characters to resist the oppressive practices of the day. As a child, Alyson had not been the recipient of the kind of message that the savvy maid in the movie gave to the young girl for whom she was responsible: "You are kind, you are smart, you are important." I introduced the practice of Energy Psychology (described in Chap. 7). I suggested that she incorporate "I am kind, I am smart, I am important" into the affirmation. Alyson immediately reported a notable reduction in her anxiety.

Alyson repeatedly raised issues regarding *purpose*. I asked her to read and share her reflections on the book: *A Purpose Filled Life* (Warren, 2004). I also shared a poem regarding "putting on armor" to initiate a discussion in follow-up to her comments that her life had been like an ongoing battle. Acknowledging her fatigue and need for peace, I encouraged her to give herself permission to pray for herself.

Early on, Alyson shared her curiosity about why God had allowed her to encounter so many challenges in life but expressed gratitude that while she had come close to the cliff, she had not fallen over. She viewed herself as spiritual but was reluctant to affiliate with a church. She saw herself as guilty of conduct she couldn't imagine of others, especially "church folk." She embraced the recommendation that she attend a grief and an Alcoholic Anonymous group as a supplement to her therapy. After visiting several community and church-sponsored groups, she opted to participate in a group hosted by a local church. She learned that choices she had made in her past did not make her "inferior" and began to socialize with some of the people she met. Eventually, she elected to attend weekly prayer meetings. Her informal adoption by "a church family" greatly reduced the social isolation that had been her reality for years.

One of the treatment objectives was increasing Alyson's acknowledgement of her *creativity*, her commitment to sharing her gifts with others, and success becoming the author of her next life chapter. I consistently encouraged her to allow herself the joy of investing time on her writing and art and from time to time prescribed the same as a between-session task. Alyson began the practice of reading her new creations aloud in session. Encouraged by the positive reception she received when she shared several of her poems at a poetry reading, she has begun researching approaches to publishing her work.

An ongoing focus in Alyson's therapy has been holding herself accountable for how she manages moments, hours, days when she feels less strong and hopeful. I have urged her to continue developing her hope toolkit; she recently e-mailed me a link to a powerfully inspiring YouTube video. It sits in her toolbox alongside secular songs with a message, her favorite spirituals, an instrumental jazz piece, a list of her favorite scriptures, a picture of her mother, a card with the inscription..."When I don't know what to do, remember: We serve a God who is omniscient (infinitely wise), omnipresent (present everywhere), and omnipotent (all powerful)," and other hope resources she has collected over time.

Alyson's investment in multiple ongoing hope practices has benefited her in small and large ways. She announced her newly found conclusion that snuggling with her cat and stuffed animals were not a substitute for human connection. She began scheduling regular face time contact with her siblings and extended family, including a new baby who brings her great joy. She reconnected with her stepdad and maintains hope he will abstain from alcohol but accepts the limits of what she can do to control his choices.

Alyson had been and remains a regular shopper at a thrift store not far from my office. A clear marker of her progress in valuing herself was clearly marked by a shopping trip she allowed herself to purchase an outfit from a regular department store and her investment in her first vacation as an adult. She enjoyed herself to the extent she has been contemplating going bungee jumping for her next venture. She began taking better care of her plants and investing more time communing with nature. She struggles still but reported recent progress decluttering her kitchen and throwing out expired food. She also has become more attentive to opening and attending to her mail.

Alyson put these accomplishments into perspective by sharing with me a printed summary of the Spoon Theory (Writings of a Chronically Ill Anthropologist, 2016) and summarized it as follows: "every task in life requires using a certain number of spoons. The number of spoons involved in performing a task varies from person to person and is contingent on context. When one has a chronic condition, one may be able to get some of the same tasks accomplished as before the illness. But completion of an ordinary task requires using more spoons than were required before the illness." Alyson was taking stock of how far she had come and expressed gratitude that, "through God's grace," she was taking charge of her life.

Alyson still has days when she struggles with loving herself, accepting the reality of abuse she recalls with her body memory and unconscious mind, and giving up the "why" question, but she has come a long way from where she started. She no longer takes psychotropic medications. Not so surprisingly, diagnostic medical tests revealed no medical bases for her complaints of abdominal pain. The pain has subsided.

More recently, Alyson proudly reported that she no longer needed to bring her stuffed animals to her sessions and she had given away her treasured play tea sets. Without prodding, she had written letters to her mom, dad, and ex-husband. Over several sessions dedicated to this agenda, she proudly read them aloud to me, owning her truth and articulating feelings she hadn't previously allowed herself to think, less dare give voice to.

I consider myself blessed to witness Alyson's courage, commitment, resilience, and ongoing recovery process (Killian, Hernandez-Wolfe, Engstrom, & Gangsei, 2017). She is a living testimony to the power of hope. She offered this metaphor, with a smile, for where she now finds herself in her healing journey: "I'm working on seeing more than the blues in the rainbow."

Hope and Healing in Community-Based Interventions

The issue of hope and hopelessness is so pervasive that it begs for attention at a preventive as well as clinical level. Here I briefly describe a preventive intervention that draws upon the premise that inspiring hope by fostering connections with cultural values and traditions is essential to transformative healing.

Aware that many youth magnify violence prevention to the status of undoable and outside their control, my colleague, Charles Etta Sutton, and I developed the SANKOFA Violence Prevention Program (Hines & Sutton, 1998). SANKOFA has a universal application but particular resonance for youth who have been marginalized in society, their parents, and educators/youth service professionals who serve them. SANKOFA is a word of West African origins that means reaching back to the wisdom of the past in order to move forward. The goal of the intervention is to equip youth with the knowledge, attitudes, skills, confidence, and motivation to minimize their risk for involvement in violence, victimization owing to violence, and other negative behaviors, such as alcohol and other drug use. The intervention promotes resilience and survival in difficult and even life-threatening situations.

A key premise undergirding SANKOFA is that healthy functioning is closely linked to active use of principles that define what one stands for and how one behaves within an oppressive context. SANKOFA is distinguished by the attention given up-front and throughout the program to supporting youth in translating and reinforcing the use of traditional African values (Karenga, 1988) to negotiate modern life challenges. Dubbed the 7Cs, the program aims to promote (1) *Consciousness*—a clear awareness of one's dreams, purpose, feelings, thoughts, beliefs, family and cultural heritage, and potential, as well as obstacles to self- and group actualization; (2) *Connectedness*—unity, a sense of interrelationship with family as well as larger kin network and community; (3) *Caring*—ability to protect, support, and show concern for the safety of one's family and the larger group, a belief in giving back; (4) *Competence toward one's purpose*—developing to one's fullest potential; (5) *Conduct*—engaging in right behavior, teaching others how to do so, the ability to forgive and resolve past injustices with one another; (6) *Creativity*—using originality, inventiveness, imagination, intuition, and artistic abilities to transform pain into meaning and hope; and (7) *Courage*—demonstrating the spiritual strength to withstand adversity and to achieve one's goals: to live up to the examples of one's ancestors.

We engage youth and accomplish the training objectives by employing a variety of teaching strategies including mini-lectures, case studies, experiential exercises, games, group discussions, peer-directed learning, modeling, and behavioral rehearsal. We use proverbs, repetitive reference to traditional values, scenarios that portray relevant and familiar situations, messages of resistance, video clips from popular movies, culture-based rituals (e.g., the talking circle) and symbolic objects (i.e., ankh), and a group motto to enhance the cultural relevance and credibility of the program.

The results from a three-year, quasi-experimental study of SANKOFA support the efficacy of the program, which has since been designated a culturally tailored, evidence-based program (Substance Abuse & Mental Health Service's National Registry of Evidence-Based Programs and Practices, 2017). The program participants and the staff who work with them on the front lines have convinced us not only of the power of hope and the value of connecting with the wisdom of those who came before us; they have taught us about the value of connectedness to community in the here and now! Systems thinkers have much to contribute to bridging the gap between what we know and what is happening on the frontlines to help individuals, families, and communities to flourish!

Working Across Differences

Hope is central to spirituality, religion, and therapy. Many therapists do not feel prepared to deal with spirituality and religion. There are many reasons: The integration of spirituality and religion into clinical practice has often been dealt with abstractly, if at all, in our training. This feeds into the notion that these issues fit in separate and distinct boxes. Unfamiliarity breeds discomfort. Therapists may not be familiar with the beliefs, values, and language used in a particular religious tradition. Many therapists interpret the mandate to be "neutral" in transactions with clients to mean that they should avoid discussions about spirituality and religion. Some fear they will abuse their power and influence clients toward adoption of their own viewpoints. Other therapists perceive religion with suspicion because of the ways it has been used to sanction oppression. There are also times when mental health issues are rooted in religious beliefs or experiences (Walsh, 2009).

Clearly, to ignore the interrelationship among mind, body, and spirit is to draw an artificial distinction that distances us from our clients. Although we can abuse our influence, the truth is that we convey messages through our omissions as well as through what we say and do in therapy. Although many clients prefer therapists who share their beliefs and values, the bottom-line concern for many is having someone with whom they can talk openly without being judged. A therapist may have beliefs that are dissonant with a client's, or the therapist and client may share common beliefs. In either instance, it is possible for therapists to be empathic, creative, and capable of facilitating hope, resilience, and healing. Greeting clients with openness to learning about them and respecting their beliefs, values, and practices is the starting place for discovering commonalities of experience that transcend differences.

Working with clients who are struggling to stay hopeful can be challenging! I often see cues of my own mounting frustration and helplessness as a signal that I need to be more compassionate with these clients and, potentially, with myself. When I encounter a moment, hour, or day when I grant myself the privilege, in the words of Fanny Lou Hamer, "to be tired of being tired", I eventually remind myself that I am not dependent and my clients are not dependent on my insights. We can benefit from the extraordinary gifts passed on by those who came before us!

When working with administrators and frontline practitioners in larger systems (i.e., education, juvenile justice, and mental health) that serve vulnerable populations, I often introduce a structured exercise during which I ask the participants to explore some of the same "hope" questions that I ask clients to explore in order to solicit their hope, faith, and resilience stories. I continue to be amazed at how few have invested in looking in the mirror and asking: Who am I? What do I believe? How do I practice hope? How can I use myself in the helping encounter to help clients find the will to pick themselves up when life knocks them down? My experience is that the participants as well as I find the dialogues revealing, helpful, and humbling as we learn about ourselves, each other, and the hope and resilience of those we seek to help.

Drawing on Spirit to Act in the Face of Despair

For those who are most vulnerable in our society, the reality is that they have come face to face with overwhelming situations, hopelessness, and despair before and will likely confront such scenarios again. There is an anecdotal evidence base drawn from the "laboratory of everyday life" that people have the capacity to overcome great odds when they have the conviction that pursuit of their dreams is worthwhile, even if hard, and when they draw on their spirituality and the wisdom and love of those past, present, and future. When we choose to use this knowledge in our work as therapists and prevention practitioners, we greatly increase the potential to help our clients to have aha moments that can lead to their empowerment and transformation.

There is an African proverb that says: To know and not to act is not to know! My grandfather's prayer remains timeless and relevant.... *Open our eyes to see, open our minds to understand, open our ears to hear, open our hearts to embrace*.... The spiritual dimension matters! It is a gift to our clients and a gift to therapists as we seek to support them in navigating their life journeys.

References

Akinyele, M. (2008). Once they come: Testimony therapy and healing questions for African American couples. In M. McGoldrick & K. Hardy (Eds.), *Re-visioning family therapy: Race, culture and gender in clinical practice* (2nd ed., pp. 356–366). New York: The Guilford Press.

Bennett, L. (1991, February). *Voices of the past* (pp. 120–122). Ebony.

Bergin, A. E. (1991). Values and religious issues in psychotherapy and mental health. *American Psychologist, 46*(4), 394–403.

Cooper-Lewter, N., & Mitchell, H. (1991). *Soul theology: The heart of American black culture.* Nashville, TN: Abingdon Press.

Copage, E. (2005). *Black pearls.* New York: Morrow.

Elliott Griffith, M., & Griffith, J. (2002). Addressing spirituality in its clinical complexities: Its potential for healing, its potential for harm. *Journal of Family Psychotherapy, 13*(1-2), 167–194.
Freire, P. (1994). *The pedagogy of hope*. New York: Continuum.
Hardy, H., & Laszloffy, T. A. (2008). The dynamics of a pro-racist ideology: Implications for training family therapists. In M. McGoldrick & K. Hardy (Eds.), *Re-visioning family therapy: Race, culture and gender in clinical practice* (2nd ed., pp. 225–237). New York: The Guilford Press.
Hines, P., & Sutton, C. (1998). *SANKOFA: A violence prevention and life skills curriculum*. Newark, NJ: University of Medicine & Dentistry of New Jersey.
Jackson, V. (2012). *Transforming powerlessness into power*. Available from microtraining: Alexander St. Press, from http://vstr.beta.alexaderstreet.com/index.pho?a=filmDetail&filmID=4038
Karenga, M. (1988). *The African American holiday of Kwanza: A celebration of family community and culture*. Los Angeles, CA: University of Sankore Press.
Killian, K., Hernandez-Wolfe, P., Engstrom, D., & Gangsei, D. (2017). Development of the vicarious resilience scale (vrs): A measure of positive effects of working with trauma survivors. *Psychological Trauma: Theory, Research, Practice, and Policy, 9*(1), 23–31.
Madsen, W. (2014). *Collaborative helping: A strengths framework for home-based services*. Hoboken, NJ: Wiley.
McGoldrick, M., & Hines, P. (2007). Hope: The far side of despair. In C. Flaskas, I. McCarthy, & J. Sheehan (Eds.), *Hope and despair in narrative and family therapy* (pp. 51–62). New York: Routledge.
Newport, F. (2016). *Most Americans still believe in God*. Downloaded February 26, 2017, from http://www.gallup.com/poll/193271/americans-believe-god.aspx
Pinderhughes, E. (1989). *Understanding race, ethnicity and power*. New York: The Free Press.
Riley, D. (1993). *My soul looks back, 'less I forget*. New York: Harper Collins.
SANKOFA Youth Violence Prevention Program. (2017). *Substance Abuse & Mental Health Service's National Registry of Evidence-Based Programs and Practices*, from https://www.samhsa.gov/nrepp
Vanzant, I. (1993). *Acts of faith*. New York: Simon & Schuster.
Velez, D. O. (2017, Sunday February 5). *Daily Kos. How black women helped shape history and today's democratic party*. Retrieved from http://www.dailykos.com/stories/2017/2/5/1627178/-How-black-women-helped-shape-history-and-today-s-Democratic-Party?detail
Walsh, F. (2009). Religion, spirituality, and the family. In F. Walsh (Ed.), *Spiritual resources in family therapy* (2nd ed., pp. 3–30). New York: The Guilford Press.
Warren, R. (2004). *The purpose-driven life: What on earth am I here for?* Grand Rapids, MI: Zondervan.
Weingarten, K. (2007). Hope in a time of global despair. In C. Flaskas, I. McCarthy, & J. Sheehan (Eds.), *Hope and despair in narrative and family therapy* (pp. 13–23). New York: Routledge.
Writings of a Chronically Ill Anthropologist. (2016). *Understanding chronic illness: What is the spoon theory and why is it important?* Chronic illness, coping & critique, from https://illness-and-intersectionality.com/2016/04/08/what-is-the-spoon-theory-understanding-chronic-illness/

Harnessing Spirituality Within Traditional Healing Systems: A Personal Journey

Hugo Kamya

Introduction

As clinicians, if we are to ask our clients to grapple with and explore their own connections to spirituality, we must be willing to do likewise. To work effectively and ethically with our clients, we must recognize how our own backgrounds, experiences with and perceptions of spirituality and religion, affect our thoughts and our work. As a clinician, an academic, a teacher, and a writer, my personal history and experiences with spirituality influence my work with clients and my thoughts on these topics, in conscious and unconscious ways. My work with clients, predominantly African immigrants who have arrived in the USA after escaping war and political violence, has explored a number of issues ranging from spiritual practices and rituals as forms of worship to metaphysical and mystical ways of being as they seek to find a sense of purpose and meaning of life experiences. In my view, these are invitations to enter into the scared spaces of our work with our clients.

In many parts of the world, and especially in many African societies, religion and spirituality are closely linked and spirituality may be regarded as an extension of religion (Mugisha, Hjelmeland, Kinyanda, & Knizek, 2013). Religion and spirituality may help people to deal specifically with illness by providing a "cognitive framework that can reduce suffering and increase one's purpose and meaning in life" (Kagimu et al., 2013); when people commit themselves to serving God or their higher power through service to others, it may function to divert attention away from their own problems and instill in them a greater sense of self-worth (Kagimu et al., 2013).

H. Kamya (✉)
School of Social Work, Simmons College, Boston, MA, USA

Boston Institute for Culturally Affirming Practices, Boston, MA, USA
e-mail: hugo.kamya@simmons.edu

D. Trimble (ed.), *Engaging with Spirituality in Family Therapy*, AFTA SpringerBriefs in Family Therapy, https://doi.org/10.1007/978-3-319-77410-7_5

Religion and spirituality are considered to be the most central facets of African heritage and the strongest social forces in Africa today, permeating all aspects of community life and playing a major role in daily decision-making (Mugisha et al., 2013). It has been suggested that spiritual explanations consistent with one's world-view—such as those invoked by the Baganda—enable patients to make meaning of their psychotic experiences in ways that promote social relatedness and cohesion, while the imposition of a purely psychiatric explanatory model has the potential to undermine the "sociocentric model of healing currently engaged in within the community" (Teuton, Bentall, & Dowrick, 2007). This has numerous implications for mental health treatment, given that embracing spiritual and religious frameworks has been found to have a positive influence on both the nature and prognosis of mental illness.

My Own Spiritual Foundations

My own background combines several intersecting narratives, each with inter-nested connections. First and foremost, I see myself as a child of two Ugandan parents who were raised to be strongly religious. My mother's father was Protestant, but she grew up near a Catholic convent and at some point she considered becoming a nun. My father, on the other hand, was mentored by the Mill Hill Missionaries, who schooled him in strong religious values. He too considered becoming a priest. From a very early age, church was very important to my parents and they worked hard to develop faith values in their children. The Christian tradition in which we grew up permeated our work and everyday life. Looking back now, I wonder if this very schooling in a Christian tradition was a form of oppression that my whole being sought to break away from. One memory of this oppressive experience is the way our schooling put missionaries on a pedestal. We were expected to revere them and to serve them. Each day, some of us cleaned their premises and there was no expectation of remuneration. We were lucky if they gave us a piece of bread from their tables that were full of plenty.

My parents made sure we said our prayers and engaged in devotional practices such as praying the rosary, novenas, and praying the Way of the Cross. They sent us to Catholic schools and made sure that we played with other Catholic children. Unfortunately, because of Uganda's religious history, strong suspicions existed between Protestants and Catholics. Since we lived near a seminary, we encountered many young men who aspired to a life of priesthood. At some point, I too contemplated becoming a priest. Looking back, I do not know if it was the life of these young seminarians that attracted me to priesthood, or if I myself also felt a call. Today as I reflect on this, I wonder if indeed the calling can be understood to be the choices that unfolded in my life.

The detention of my father after he had disappeared for several years was one such event. One evening, a group of armed men stormed into our family's house while we were having dinner. The intruders wore military uniforms and carried guns. They demanded to see "the man of the house"; they were looking for my father. My father ran into the bedroom and the men followed. A gunshot was fired. After what seemed a very long time the men walked out of the bedroom with the threat that they would return. We sat motionless, praying for courage. Then, quietly, we walked into the bedroom. There was a *crack in the window* and a streak of blood on the floor. There was no sign of our father. His disappearance left our family with few options beyond hoping for his return. With my mother as the sole breadwinner, our family turned to faith to find a place of comfort and solace. Our faith became the backbone of our life.

Another important influence was the life of my brother, Joseph whose struggles through childhood, adolescence, and young adulthood came to embody my family's own self-understanding. With the realization that Joseph was hearing impaired, unable to speak, and struggling with many challenges, I came to appreciate the blessings in my life and family. Joseph's difficulties with communication alienated him from all of us as a family, perhaps including himself. His inability to speak was a silence that affected us all, and came with a costly pain as we all struggled to make sense of it. It also revealed yet another aspect of the many silences we lived through as a family. Unfortunately, his challenges were not diagnosed early in his life. He struggled with anger and angry outbursts that he often unleashed on all of us, his younger siblings.

My life was also profoundly shaped by the narrative of Uganda as a "colony" of Britain. Growing up in a postcolonial country, I struggled to understand the "benevolence" of Uganda's colonial masters and their sanitized oppression. For my country, colonialism found other names that justified it. Uganda was a "protectorate" rather than a "colony" of Britain. When repressive regimes succeeded colonial imperialism, there was little incentive to resist those who claimed to be our protectors. On the one hand, religion that came with colonization was oppressive. On the other hand, traditional religion provided a sense of comfort. Traditional religion and cultural traditions of harmony and preservation of life grounded me in the need to build understanding. As a member of the largest tribe in my country, I felt a sense of power that was checked by the helplessness I felt throughout postcolonial Uganda. This enabled me to understand the powerlessness embedded in retaliatory discourses (Kamya & Trimble, 2002). Perhaps even more pressing for me was the anger I intensely felt as I struggled to construct "the other" in those who oppressed my family. Although this anger gave me a means to deal with my pain, I could not live, and chose not to be, consumed by my anger. A path through restorative justice became an opportunity to embrace this challenge. This has become my faith and hope especially in the face of struggle and pain. The *crack in the window* became a metaphor through which I felt a sense of hope and deliverance.

The years that followed the disappearance of my father were harrowing as all of us, as a family, sought to find some sense of meaning in the events that had befallen us. What made it even more senseless was the fact that we could not identify who our enemies were. So, we lived with this lack of knowing and uncertainty that good could ever come out of it. Fear, anger, frustration, and confusion engulfed our entire being. These emotions created a strong sense of silence we lived with. The only thing that kept us going was the hope that one day our father would return to us.

The *crack in the window* soon came to have important symbolic meaning for me. The day the intruders invaded our home left an indelible mark in my life. The events of that day and those that followed created both chaos and opportunity. The *crack in the window* at first shattered my hopes of ever seeing my father again. However, it ultimately provided me a sense of hope and determination to live on. It was not until much later that we learned the fate of our father. For years, we sat, we waited, and we hoped. Our waiting took on a new meaning and perseverance that provided us a sense of purpose. This waiting and not knowing became the "positive motivational state… derived [from a] sense of successful agency" (Snyder et al., 1991, p. 287). It has also become an important lens through which I have come to view my work with immigrant and refugee populations. As we waited for the return of our father, we prayed and sang songs of hope. My mother took on a job at a local training institute for ministry. She worked long hours washing and cleaning rooms and dishes. As siblings, we pitched in to take care of house chores. Two youngest siblings went to live with our grandmother 50 miles away. We took turns to go visit them on weekends while our mother worked to support us. At times, we survived on one meal a day. Regardless of the challenges, we were determined to survive.

As I discuss spirituality and integrate the spiritual into my own clinical practice, I do so from the foundation of these experiences. But, I have also wondered about myself as a spiritual being who is located beyond what my parents have taught me, the political hegemony that I, my family, and many others lived through. I have often thought about that defining moment in my family's life. I have asked myself many questions. What kept us together? Why did we not fall apart? Why had the events of that night remained so significant in the face of what we had together as a family? But, I also ask myself other questions. How come we survived this ordeal? Why did we survive when many other families did not?

These questions catapulted me into meanings that are foundational anchors of my life. I have come to think deeply about my spiritual roots and ask myself even more questions: Who am I as a spiritual being? What sustains my sense of being? How does myself as a spiritual being intimately relate to myself as a human being? Indeed, the words of Teilhard de Chardin ring true. I ask myself if I am a human being having a spiritual experience or if I am spiritual being having a human experience (Teilhard de Chardin, 1955). I also wonder about the spiritual import of the practices and rituals that were part of my growing up as African. My life as an immigrant and as a refugee echoes the lives of many immigrants and refugees that I work with. I know my work with refugees and immigrants often echoes my own story. I often hear reverberations of my own story as I seek to make meaning of their own story.

One such a story is my work with a young man from Southern Sudan who traveled a long distance looking for his family. His journeys took him into Ethiopia before he ended up in Uganda and finally in Kakuma refugee camp in Kenya. He told his story with so much grief and pain describing the challenges he encountered along the way. He could not trust the people he encountered on his journey. He felt

God had abandoned him. Yet, he also knew that he was alive while many of his people were killed. He struggled with all kinds of feelings in him: fear, uncertainty, sadness, anger, and more. He lacked a country he could call his own and kept asking himself questions: who am I and where do I belong? What does the future hold for me? And whose future is it?

This young man's story reminded me of my story. The political turmoil in Uganda led me to flee my country into Kenya. I traveled at night, hitching rides from strangers and walking on foot as I crossed into Kenya with very few belongings. The journey across the border would not allow me to carry much luggage for fear of detection and the uncertainties that lay ahead. I traveled in a minibus with at least 13 or 14 fellow travelers. None of us said a word to each other. Although it was clear we were all escaping Uganda, none dared to mention our final destination or why we were traveling at all. I still vividly remember sitting nervously in that minibus without daring even to make eye contact with another passenger. Everyone was suspect. No one could be trusted. As much as I wanted to connect with someone on that bumpy ride, I had to maintain a distance to ensure that no one asked me questions or recognized my nervousness. Our distance from each other, when tightly squeezed in such a small vehicle, was a necessary protection.

At various roadblocks, soldiers would pull us out of the vehicle; soldiers would yell at us in Swahili, a language none of us spoke, but which many of us identified with intimidation and brutality. Our fate depended on the whims of the soldiers who manned checkpoints. Some people were hauled out of vehicles, interrogated, pushed around, and eventually released before the vehicle took off. Others were not as lucky. They were hit with gun butts and threatened with barrels pointed at their heads. The name on one's identification card often sealed one's fate. If you belonged to a tribe that was not in favor of the government, you were a prime suspect. We were all trying to escape fear, intimidation, and uncertainty that came with these wars. We also lived distrusting everyone else, including people who were supposed to be our neighbors.

The Life of Immigrants and Refugees

Most of my work has been with African immigrants. Although some immigrants come to the USA for economic and educational reasons, more have had to flee their homelands, often against their will and under horrific conditions. When they arrive, they find that the skills that assured them economic stability in their countries of origin are not valued here. Moreover, immigration laws and economic difficulties prevent family members from joining their relatives in the USA Families may have to shoulder the burden of bringing in others who, without appropriate immigration papers, fear deportation. Parents work long hours leaving them little time and energy to pass on to their children the cultural traditions, values, and rituals that have sustained them in their home context.

Most immigrants experience a deep sense of loss of their culture associated with loss of language, not only for themselves but also for their children. Parents lament their inability to communicate with their children as they could in their home countries, and feel a deep sense of regret when their Americanized children fail to learn their language. Prolonged separation of family members often creates gaps in shared family history. Family members become strangers to each other, leading to major strains and disappointments. For many, losing contact with loved ones can affect connections within families. Most frightening of all is the fear of deportation for those who have arrived with no proper documentation.

One young man from Uganda reported that he wished so much to pass on to his children his culture, spiritual, and religious beliefs and practices but lacked the structures he enjoyed in his home country. "My children will never be able to worship in the same way that my parents taught me," he lamented. He also felt so alienated from his own cultural rites of passages that he could not provide in the same way to his children.

The relocation of immigrants typically awakens fear, depression, and insecurity along with excitement and hope. Immigrants must adjust both attitudinally and behaviorally to a new culture and environment. Immigrants often have difficulties locating housing and jobs. Poverty and unfamiliarity with the US social cues leave them vulnerable to crime and in some cases to exploitation by the host culture. Anti-immigrant sentiments have also exacerbated the life of many people as they seek refuge in the USA.

There are others for whom even escape from war in their home country to the USA does not offer any promise of safety. A 50-year-old man who escaped the killing fields of the Democratic Republic of Congo was plagued by nightmares in his sleep and was constantly reminded of the killing fields when he opened the daily newspaper. When he sought a church to find a community that he hoped would provide him some comfort and connectedness, he instead found huge divisions among his own country folks, reminders of the intense divisions back in his country of origin. Often these experiences are felt with a strong sense of betrayal.

My work with refugees and immigrants has uncovered important considerations for me, including appreciation of the spiritual connections to my core being. My spiritual connections are anchored in my African traditional religious beliefs. Similarly, I have come to appreciate my family in the context of these beliefs. These traditional religious beliefs comfort many Africans facing life's hardships and permeate all areas of life. African beliefs are rooted in the power of both the natural and the spiritual worlds. These worlds are experienced as both "instrumental and metaphysical" (Rivett & Street, 2001). Spiritual powers, which include the supreme god, other divinities, the spirits, and one's ancestors, are invoked and prayed to, and sometimes libations are poured to honor them. They constitute the religious systems through which most people understand themselves. Over the years, I have come to understand these religious systems in contexts including history, economics, politics, and colonialism among other powerful influences on life.

I have come to appreciate the beliefs of my African ancestors for whom spirits reside in the mountains, rivers, lakes, trees, rocks, and other objects. These natural objects are seen as carrying extraordinary powers in life and people's worldview. Unfortunately, many traditions and rituals that Africans have built around these natural objects have been dismissed by major monotheistic religious traditions as pagan or uncouth. Indeed, in most cases the monotheistic West has placed African religions at the lowest rank of the religious evolution toward monotheism, below Christianity, Judaism, and Islam. This perception of superiority rooted in colonial imperialism created an uneasy tension between African spiritual beliefs and the major monotheistic religions. Yet, as I work with many immigrants and refugees they remain key anchors of their own self-understanding.

My sense of self as a spiritual being is rooted in my being as part of a religious tradition which permeates all aspects of my life as an African. I embrace all the mystical powers of the universe. I believe nothing happens by chance. I think of the mysterious mystical powers that are always operative in my life. In some ways, I am aware of these mystical powers; in other ways, I am not. My belief in the divine or spiritual beings translates into a commitment to worship in varied forms, whether in open, private, or public forum that sustain a sense of connection, purpose, and meaning. Worship is a form of prayer that helps me to find my own sense of connection to self and to the community around me. My African beliefs have also helped me to realize my own deep connection to community. These views have helped me to begin to dismantle the dominant Christian discourse that has plagued and created hegemony over my African traditions. As my clients have described their journeys, I have listened closely to the oppressive discourses that have enslaved them and habituated them into submission.

I have also come to value the world of Africans that is populated with spiritual beings, spirits, and the living–dead (Mbiti, 1990) all of whom play a major role in the culture of Africans. Many Africans find their sense of purpose and meaning in the relationships that individuals or community have with the spiritual beings, all of whom are seen as guides to a well-lived life. Some Africans consider major objects in nature, like the sun or moon, as spiritual beings. Indeed, many Africans revere these objects of nature. They name children after these objects out of respect and to seek protection from them. Protection provides them comfort, connectedness, and control. Most Africans hold their belief in powerful spiritual beings with reverence and transcendence. Spirits guide family structure, child rearing practices, and indeed the entire life cycle. Africans believe in preserving harmony with these spirits. When parents lose control of their children, spirits are invoked to provide guidance and solutions. Among my tribal group, the Baganda of Uganda, the living–dead, who are believed to dwell around homesteads, are considered to be benevolent spirits. Africans live out their spirituality through elaborate dances that invoke these spirits. In some groups, people enter into trances, meditative states believed to connect them to spiritual beings. Spirituality and spiritual beings are also intimately connected to the notion of community.

Community Identity as a Spiritual Identity

Community relates to spiritual identity. Africans believe in communal identity, involving both the living and the dead. Mbiti (1990) noted that African personal identity is found in the context of their community's identity. One African proverb found in many languages states: "I am because we are." Africans try to integrate their sacred and secular into one harmonious, cooperative, and communal orientation without formal distinction between the sacred and the secular, between the religious and the nonreligious, and between the spiritual and the material areas of life (Mbiti, 1990).

As spiritual beings, Africans organize this sense of community around major events of the family life cycle, frequently engaging others in planning celebrations around births or marriages, funerals, and mourning rituals. Relatives and friends will travel long distances to attend these key moments. Elaborate meals with displays of traditional ethnic foods mark family get-togethers. These rituals underscore the spiritual beliefs and practices of our lives as Africans. My work with African immigrants and refugees has sought to connect to the depth of meaning and purpose that these rituals and practices address. They underscore a connection to the past, the present, and the future. They evoke the sacred in the life of the community.

These beliefs and practices have guided my self-knowledge in my work with immigrant and refugee populations. I have often reflected on the meaning of these formative experiences and their relationship to my life as a spiritual being. In the same way, I have reflected on how my life as a spiritual being with this spiritual legacy of my traditions intersects with the lives of immigrants and refugees as spiritual beings. They have also helped me to enter the world of my clients as I have sought to find a sense of meaning and purpose in the seeming hopelessness and helplessness that surrounds them.

I value the history of ancestors, the practices, and beliefs that have held me as an African and as an immigrant in a new world. My practice is anchored and guided by a commitment to understand the depth of loss and disruption suffered by refugee and immigrant populations. As a group, they are negotiating many life losses through their immigrant and refugee journey. For my part, I have come to learn that their journey has been a search for renewal, healing, and harmony.

The Story of Mot

The story of Mot captures what I have come to understand as my relationship with my own spiritual core. It is also emblematic of the lives of refugee and immigrant populations in my clinical work. Mot was one of the many refugee children from Sudan who came to be known as the "Lost Boys" (a term they disliked, since they did not think of themselves as lost). Mot, who lived with a foster family, was referred to me for therapy because of increasing behavior problems at school.

The story of Mot captures the struggle of his relationship with a higher power, his search for purpose and meaning, and healing in his life. Mot, 19, comes from the Sudanese Dinka tribe. At a very early age, he spent days roaming the devastated war fields in Southern Sudan, crossing several rivers and chased several times by wild animals. He spent days hiding from various warring groups, often without any food. He ended up crossing into Northern Uganda and finally settled into the refugee camp at Kakuma. His is a story of great pain and suffering, dotted throughout with questions such as: "Why did this happen to me?" "What about my brothers and sisters, what happened to them?" "Why did the gods do this to us?" Why do brothers kill each other?" "How can I forgive them as we have been taught by *Deng*?" (a spirit God in the indigenous spiritual tradition of the Dinka tribal group).

These are essentially spiritual questions with psychological and existential challenges. They speak to important issues in his relationship with God and search for purpose and meaning in life. Mot's questions echo those of other refugee children who have seen and been wounded by so much evil. They question and search for answers as they attempt to make meaning of their lives. In their struggle to deal with the psychological impact of these events, they try to make sense of senseless atrocities.

In fleeing from their country, these refugees have had to overcome the traumas of war, persecution, torture, and inhumane treatment. Their sense of basic trust and security has been shattered. Their struggle also includes trying to understand themselves in the context of challenges faced by most immigrants in adaptation to a new life in a foreign land far from home. The migration process involves multiple losses, including loss of kin and social support systems, identity, belief systems, and status (Falicov, 2002). Separated from familiar and cherished people, places, and possessions, refugees often go through prolonged transitions. They must begin to build new reconfigured identities and lives, learning new customs, language, norms, and values. Host societies present challenges of loneliness and alienation. African refugees and Muslims, in particular, often face racism and discrimination. In short, immigrants, and especially refugees, experience varying levels of physical, psychological, sociological, emotional, and spiritual/religious rootlessness.

For many refugees like Mot, attention to spiritual resources has been key. These resources have included the use of prayer and metaphor to build toward healing. Over time, I have come to appreciate their value for healthy integration of life. Both prayer and metaphor have come to represent the instrumental and the metaphysical in the lives of immigrants and refugees. I will discuss prayer and metaphor in relation to my work with Mot.

Prayer as a Form of Communion and Healing

Across cultures and religions, most people turn to some form of prayer in the face of adversity (Walsh, 2008). The value of prayer for health, well being, and healing has been well documented (Dossey, 1993; Koenig, McCullough, & Larson, 2001).

For refugees and immigrants, prayer is a major spiritual resource, both within communal services and in personal practice. On a number of occasions, Mot has spoken about the value of prayers and rituals in his life. Mot was raised Christian and he has had to find some way of integrating his Christian upbringing with his African traditional prayer worship. Repetitive prayer, recitation, and chanting have been part of Mot's prayer life. This exercise has often created a centering practice for Mot in which he is able to recollect himself when he is overwhelmed or flooded with painful wartime memories. He has shared with me his ability to say certain words and phrases that he repeats to himself as a way of finding comfort. In my work with Mot, I have sought to understand with him how he uses prayer to express his faith, his work, and his life as a religious person. When he utters prayer he experiences various transformations, some of which reveal new identities and life possibilities. For instance, he has named himself as a warrior who will always act on his own behalf, underscoring a new sense of self-agency.

For Mot, prayer has carried with it a protective power, one that offers him protection from evil and misfortune. Prayer has also strengthened his conviction and determination to overcome his life difficulties. At times, his prayer has also been a form of admission of his vulnerability or an assertion of some sense of control over his life. When Mot has used prayer to connect to his existence, I have also observed his wish to enter into communication with and willingness to surrender to something larger than himself. Thus, as he shares with me in our conversations his use of prayer, it has become an opportunity for us to explore his growth in awareness of his own condition. It has also become a way of connecting to others, like family members and friends, whom he cannot touch or reach at this time in his life. He feels their spiritual presence as he mentions them in his prayers. Prayer has become a transitional object for him. His prayers have been both vocal and silent. In vocal prayer, he has openly prayed for loved ones left behind or those who have died or been killed. Remembering them in prayer has been a way of honoring them.

As well as a sense of connection, refugees also speak at times about their sense of disconnection from loved ones and from protective communities. Mot has often talked about "those people who lied to me," referring to families that took him in as he trekked south to escape the killing fields of Sudan. He recalls on many occasions people who offered him and others a "home" but ended up abusing them, placing them under hard manual labor to earn their upkeep. He often talks about living with a sense of betrayal and with the suspicion that no one really cared. That leads him to question whether God can be completely trusted.

While prayers seeking deliverance and protection tend to preoccupy the life of refugees and immigrants I work with, other prayers acknowledge with gratitude God's presence and role in taking away their troubles. Many have talked about being created by God and owing their very existence to God. The belief in a caring and loving God often helps to sustain them in their tribulations. It has therefore been important to ask about their perception of God and God's willingness to step in when life becomes difficult. Such a sense of hopefulness is no clearer than in Mot's own words:

> Sometimes, we crossed the same river two or three times to escape being noticed by the enemy. We kept running. We did not know who we were running away from. We could not trust anyone. It was very scary. Some of the children belonged to the enemy and they reported on us. We were too scared to sleep at night. We wondered what would happen to us. We hated them and I suppose they hated us. We hoped God who created all of us would save us from danger. And God did!

Aylward Shorter is an anthropologist and a priest who worked in Africa. In his book, *Prayer in the religious traditions of Africa*, he cites the work of Fran Heiler, *Prayer: A study in the history and psychology of religion.* Heiler understood prayer as a communication and as a communion of the social human relations (Shorter, 1975). For Heiler, prayer is an awakening into one's consciousness. It is a dimension of life that transcends and reinterprets every social relationship and social experience. Whether uttered formally or informally, it also serves a number of social purposes.

Shorter outlines 15 themes recurrent in African prayer, subsumed under four major categories: relational themes, situational themes, purposive themes, and universal themes. One relational sub-theme is that of divine governance: in God's master mind, God both protects, and challenges. Mot's words echo this both/and paradox, revealing both a sense of despair regarding the challenges, but also a sense of hope in God's protection and provision. In my work with Mot, I have invited him to share prayers and intercessions in his own life. Listening to his prayers, I have heard some of Shorter's themes. Together, we have delved into the wishes his prayers express, the values they hold for him and the direction they point toward. I have also wondered with him about the commitments his prayers are making in these utterances. What has become increasingly clear to us in our work together is the interconnectedness of these utterances for him with the community in his life. Above all, I have also begun to notice how much his current situation is related to other people in his life, the purpose and meaning in his life, and ultimately his own commitment to bigger and greater hopes for his life.

Clinical work with refugees is about exploring ways of connecting. Prayers offer one important way to reconnect refugees and immigrants with loved ones left behind. They truly serve as transitional objects. Prayers invoke relational themes in which refugees and immigrants also connect with family members who have died. Prayers are not just about intercession. They are also about honoring family members and the gifts they have given each other. Ultimately, they are about celebrating life's rites of passage. They are indeed an instrumental aspect of spirituality (Rivett & Street, 2001).

Metaphors as Conduits of Healing

Metaphor is another tool that is useful as a spiritual resource for refugees and immigrants, which I have used in my therapeutic work with them. Metaphor can be seen as a metaphysical lens with tremendous possibilities. Babits (2001) has described metaphor as holding "the inner edge of possibility." The use of metaphor can expand clinical possibilities. Metaphors often suggest more than one way of understanding reality. They provide new windows of understanding even as they leave a lot to interpretation. Metaphors are often alive and rich in meaning. For Babits (2001), metaphor is "most readily associated with image, vision, which is our most developed sense, occupying a larger area of the cerebral cortex than any other" (p. 23).

Metaphors are employed in many cultural groups, including different indigenous traditions. Among immigrant and refugee groups, metaphoric pictures seek to explain reality and mystery. Metaphors provide the living documents through which mystery unfolds. The use of metaphors to reveal and hold complexity can be a valuable spiritual resource in therapy with refugees.

Meaning making is a crucial process for recovery and resilience, particularly in the wake of trauma and loss (Walsh, 2007). Critically important are efforts to gain a "*sense of coherence*" (Walsh, 2008, 2007), through new perspectives on senseless atrocities, unbearable suffering, and overwhelming struggles: to see them as comprehensible, manageable, and meaningful challenges. Clinical work with refugees' metaphors can indeed provide that sense of coherence.

A careful exploration of metaphor, therefore, is key to therapeutic work. I have used metaphors to transcend polarized "either/or" choices in the lives of immigrants by offering a rich and complex way to understand the personal, family, and social transformations they experience and their capacity to find both/and solutions (Falicov, 2002, p. 2). For instance, viewing their new community as a "spiritual home" and "spiritual extended family" which enables refugees to feel connected without cutting off from their deep bonds with their family and culture of origin. As Falicov stresses, adaptation and wellbeing are fostered when immigrants and refugees can forge a bicultural identity, with roots in both worlds.

In my work with Mot, as with many other refugees and immigrants, I have used metaphor to provide a window of understanding into the plights in his life and his life journey ahead. Metaphors have also offered him ways to interpret important messages and to assist him in holding on even when things seem impossible. "A river flowing with joy" is one metaphor that Mot has used frequently to describe his wish in life. He has described many rivers he has crossed. "Most of these rivers were furiously angry at us. They swept everything that came our way. They carried off my cousin. We never saw him again. I would like to swim in a new river that flows with joy…" These images speak about Mot's relationship to the ordeal he went through as he traveled to find a new home. He has often depicted his own sense of peace as—"a river that flows with joy. Together, we have explored this image and found ways to expand this imagery. I have asked him how the river gives to him—what soothing he feels as he imagines the river in his life. While he recognizes the turbulence that comes with the river, he also notices the calmness of the river. Such ability to acknowledge goodness alongside tragedy has been very effective in managing moments of frustration in his life. Together, we have sat with the pain of his situation and the helplessness that comes along with it. We have also been able to sit back and unpack the resilience, and the joy that comes with it. We have been able to embrace the complexity and the simplicity that this situation presents. This exercise has provided our work opportunities to transcend into new territories.

More recently, Mot has begun to expand the river metaphor to his ongoing life challenges. A river that flows with joy holds a sense of hope for him as he constructs a new life in the USA. When things have not gone well at his school, in his foster family, and in his community, he has talked about his "river letting him down" and his wish that things were better. Although he is gaining grounding in his new home, he continues to describe his life as a "river that still flows in many different directions."

For my part in our work, I have wondered with him about other ways the river could provide more opportunities for healing. We have talked about water and its life giving force. He has described how he walked miles in his little village to fetch water that was used in his home. He remembers how the river provided habitat for fish that was food for his tribal group. The waters of the Nile also provided irrigation for their crops and farms.

We have also expanded the metaphor to seek new meanings of water and river in his life today. He now describes his life in the USA as a long river with "winding twists and turns." "Sometimes, I like them;" he says, "sometimes, I hate them." The river has become one way to unpack good days and bad days in his life.

Mot's use of metaphors is common among Africans to comprehend their world and their place in it, which are existential, spiritual matters. Many will use figures of speech because they speak to a core understanding unmatched in other more concrete or factual ways of speaking. Often these figures of speech provide a window in their self-understanding and their core beliefs. They also allow them to enter a world of transcendence.

As Mot and others have talked with such rich imagery, I have also tapped into figures of speech that express my core beliefs with the hope that I can connect to their core beliefs. In doing so, I have come to a happy realization that it is not just the figure of speech that matters, but also the very experiences that underlie them. My own life experiences and the attack on my family when I was a 10-year-old boy brought me face to face with a crack in the window, the result of a shot fired at my father as he escaped through the window. Over the years, what was once a literal crack became a metaphor for me. I have come to realize that what gives me hope is less about a particular figure of speech, the "crack in the window" which for me was a—"ray of hope"—but the events that surround that crack in the window.

Rites of Passage

Rites of passage is an African spiritual tradition that celebrates major transitions in the life of Africans. The rites of passage are markers of transitions from one moment to another. Among Africans, these moments, which include birth, naming, childhood into adolescence then youth-hood into adulthood and beyond, signal movement from one stage to another. They look forward even as they look backwards and serve as important transitional objects in the life of Africans. These stages are marked with key events as circumcision, marriages, giving birth, and celebrating life and death. They offer connection to permanence and existence. In my work with immigrants we have returned to the rites of passage that characterize their life and their self-understanding. It has been helpful to examine key moments that have helped them transition. These moments have included events such as an escape, a river crossing, a witnessing of a death or even finding oneself alive after everyone else has been killed off.

The crack in the window was one aspect in this traditional African practice—the rites of passage. My father's experience that became my family's experience helped my family to transition from one key moment to another. It was a cleansing of sorts as it allowed us to reevaluate our lives in the context of our plight. It opened us to a place we had never been bringing with it new responsibilities. Similarly, Mot's immigration journey, just like mine, were transitions into new spaces. They revealed something we were leaving behind into something new and different.

As I have described elsewhere (Kamya, 2005), no event has been more hope filled for me or given to me as the crack in the window that I noticed after armed men attacked our home, shooting at my father. I can vividly recall that each time I looked at that crack in the window I held some hope that my father was still alive and would return to us some day. Although it took many years for my prayers to be answered, the crack in the window gave me a secret joy and expectation I so badly needed. It has continued to hold hope for me both in my personal and professional life. It provides the passion to do the work. My work with African immigrants and refugees has been one of "faithful companioning" and faithful hoping as we all have sought to locate that "inner edge of possibility" within the metaphors we have consulted, and in the process, created even more metaphors that have helped to ground us in our work. These sacred spaces have become brave spaces without which my work with immigrants would be meaningless.

References

Babits, M. (2001). Using therapeutic metaphor to provide a holding environment: The inner edge of possibility. *Clinical Social Work Journal, 29*(1), 21–33.

Dossey, D. (1993). *Healing words: The power of prayer and the practice of medicine*. New York: Harper.

Falicov, C. J. (2002). Ambiguous loss: Risk and resilience in Latino immigrant families. In M. Suarez-Orozco (Ed.), *Latinos: Remaking America*. Oakland, CA: University of California Press.

Kagimu, M., Guwatudde, D., Rwabukwali, C., Kaye, S., Walakira, Y., & Ainomugisha, D. (2013). Religiosity for promotion of behaviors likely to reduce new HIV infections in Uganda: A study among Muslim youth in Wakiso District. *Journal of Religion & Health, 52*(4), 1211–1227.

Kamya, H. (2005). African immigrant families pp. 101–116. In M. McGoldrick, J. Giordano, & N. Garcia-Preto (Eds.), *Ethnicity and famil therapy* (3rd ed.). New York: Guilford Press.

Kamya, H., & Trimble, D. (2002). Response to injury: Toward ethical construction of the other. *Journal of Systemic Therapies., 21*(3), 19–29.

Koenig, H., McCullough, M. E., & Larson, D. (Eds.). (2001). *Handbook of religion and health*. New York: Oxford University Press.

Mbiti, J.S. (1990). *African religions and philosophy*. New York: Doubleday.

Mugisha, J., Hjelmeland, H., Kinyanda, E., & Knizek, B. L. (2013). Religious views on suicide among the Baganda, Uganda: A qualitative study. *Death Studies, 37*(4), 343–361.

Rivett, M., & Street, E. (2001). Connections and themes of spirituality in family therapy. *Family Process, 40*, 459–467.

Shorter, A. (1975). *Prayer in the religious traditions of Africa*. Nairobi, Kenya: Oxford University Press.

Teilhard de Chardin, P. (1955). *The phenomenon of man*. New York: Harper Perennial.

Teuton, J., Bentall, R., & Dowrick, C. (2007). Conceptualizing psychosis in Uganda: The perspective of indigenous and religious healers. *Transcultural Psychiatry, 44*(1), 79–114.

Walsh, F. (2007). Traumatic loss and major disasters: Strengthening family and community resilience. *Family Process, 46*, 207–227.

Walsh, F. (2008). *Spiritual resources in family therapy*. New York: Guilford.

The Tao As & Of Spiritual Healing: Reframing Reconciliation and Recovery

Jay T. King

Both my spiritual and my professional life emerge from the balance I found in the middle location of the Tao. I was born in the middle; the middle of the century and the middle of the year 1949, at the end of June. Perhaps it was destiny that my worldview was organized around the aggressive, asserting and yielding, dependent and independent, hard and soft, feminine and masculine.

I was the oldest of four boys raised by teenagers from the 1940s through 1960s in Cambridge, Massachusetts, working class but probably considered middle class by the time I became a teenager. My mother was a brown-skin Catholic and my father was a very light-skin Protestant Episcopalian. We were raised in a Protestant church in part because my mother was banned from her church for her choice to marry a non-Catholic. That was my earliest exposure to what I saw as self-righteous discrimination and abuse practiced by religion. My mother was also pregnant before marriage, which did not earn her any morality points in the Catholic Church. As a young teenager, I was actively involved in Sunday School, and in the church choir until late in my teens. I struggled with the social and racial turmoil of the mid 1960s while having serious doubts about the religion endorsed by my family. I sought a theology that was more inclusive, or at least less exclusive.

As I began high school in Cambridge, my parents moved me from a predominantly black technical high school for kids with a reading level below third grade, to an all-white middle class neighborhood in Newton, Massachusetts. Most of my peers and classmates were planning to attend Ivory League schools like Harvard, Brown, and Yale, and the rest were headed for MIT, Cal Tech, Stanford, and Berkeley. It was a traumatic transition for me. In my technical school in Cambridge, no one was expected to apply for college. In my new middle class school and

J. T. King (✉)
Palo Alto University, Palo Alto, CA, USA

Boston Institute for Culturally Affirming Practices, Boston, MA, USA
e-mail: jayking@paloaltou.edu

D. Trimble (ed.), *Engaging with Spirituality in Family Therapy*, AFTA SpringerBriefs in Family Therapy, https://doi.org/10.1007/978-3-319-77410-7_6

neighborhood, I was the only student who could not name a single book that I had completed before grade 9. Fortunately, I was a quiet kid who did not cause trouble and I was a very good athlete, so I survived high school and found my way into an athletic scholarship in a college on the outskirts of New York City.

During my freshman year in college, one of my favorite and most admired Christian leaders, Rev Dr. Martin Luther King, was assassinated. This event corrupted and challenged both my Christian faith and my father's belief that education was the answer to oppression and racism. Prior to 1968, I had been very much committed to becoming a professional athlete. I had also considered becoming a sports photographer, so I chose to register in college as a business major. The assassination of Dr. King triggered a search for an alternative religion, philosophy, and lifestyle. I continued to think of myself first and foremost as an athlete, but I was drawn to the philosophies of martial arts that enhanced the internal and external power of the athlete's body and mind.

Winning by Losing

As I was losing my hero, my mentor, and my religion, my prayers were answered. I discovered Taoism, embedded in my training in martial arts, Tai Chi, and Jujitsu. Here were a philosophy, spirituality, and religion that spoke to me, an orientation and a set of very clear and well-articulated values and principles that mapped and described a world view seeming to match exactly the one that I had carried around with me for years without recognizing that it had a history and a name. I discovered the substance and the meaning of Taoism and the symbolic and spiritual meaning of Yin Yang. I was intrigued by its ideas of "winning by losing," and "victory through yielding." I interpreted the ideas to mean that rigid attachment to the religious teaching of my childhood could be counterproductive, and "letting go" could expand my search for a more inclusive alternative theology.

One of the most appealing aspects of Taoism for me was that it was unequivocally inclusive, balanced, integrative, and adaptive, and its resistance to rigid righteousness was genuinely unencumbered. It was infused with humility. It was predicated on characteristics of nature, making it visible to the human eye and allowing transcendence. It encouraged study and learning as opposed to worship. It embraced contradictions while encouraging the recognition of "paradoxical compatibilities." We often conclude that certain feelings, behaviors, and beliefs are incompatible, when a more Taoist examination will allow us to discover compatibilities that were previously invisible. This is visually represented by the symbol of Yin Yang that highlights the light sphere in the larger dark space and highlights the dark sphere in the larger light space. In simple terms, the symbol suggests that what is typically seen as good also has a capacity to be bad *and* what is typically seen as bad also has the capacity to be good. Strong has the capacity to be weak and weak has the capacity to be strong and resilient. The Yin Yang can be as simple as the concept of male characteristics in females and female characteristics in males, or of the sea as a body of water that has tranquil characteristics in some parts, and violent and raging characteristics in other. "Taoism is an Eastern Philosophy that acknowledges the harmony of opposites" (Siegmann, 2000). The Tao is both the force and the surrender, the push and the yield, the Yin and the Yang.

Clinical Constructs

I sometimes use the following application of Taoism in my practice with couples who are stuck in verbal combat and cannot seem to let go of their need to win their fights and declare themselves RIGHT! "Your home work for this week is to *lose* all the fights that you will have with your partner and to take notes on how you lost the fight and what the fight was about." This assignment is typically very difficult and usually requires several weeks of in-session practice to catch hold. Once the couple has engaged in the process, several things happen.

(a) The couple begin to absorb the substance of each other's position.
(b) They recognize that there can be more than ONE right (truth) and/or that they can both be right from different perspectives and/or when looking through different lenses.
(c) The couple often find that they are fighting about trivia and that the time they put into these arguments is entirely counterproductive
(d) Most importantly, they recognize that they are putting the idea of being "right" as a priority over being a smart supportive partner, which is a critical construction when working with couples, relationships, and families.

Another form in the martial arts, Jujitsu, involves allowing your opposition to overpower itself with little if any resistance from you. This often includes *not* confronting a client but rather listening to them until they walk themselves into a corner (contradiction) and discover on their own terms that they are not able to make sense of what they are feeling, thinking, saying, or doing.

"Embracing your ignorance" is another Taoist concept, also known as "rotating from the role of teacher to role of student." The smart space may also be stupid and the stupid space may also be smart, Yin and Yang together. In clinical practice, this means retreating from the "expert" position and being a student while inviting the client to be your teacher. This is also extraordinarily effective when teaching, coaching, mentoring, and consulting.

> The essential work of the mentor is to guide others to discovering this goodness within themselves and to help them follow their integrity as they reawaken to the inner truth of who they are… "Teaching and learning are interlaced, for both mentor and mentoree have a heart 'that watches and receives.' Neither mentor or mentoree can exist without the other. They define each other…This paradoxical mystery where the duality is neutralized, this is called the Wu Ming, the nondualistic Tao. No longer can we tell whether it is the student offering himself to the teacher or the teacher offering himself to the student. We see each of the two beings mirroring the other in pure reflection. "Those who know they know not, become wise those who presume they know much, stay ignorant." (Chungliang & Lynch, 1999).

Another example of Taoist thinking in popular rhetoric is the phrase, "keep your friends close and keep your enemies closer." This seems to be a contradictory recommendation, but from the Taoist perspective it makes very good sense, "paradoxically compatible."

A client reported to me that he could not leave his abusive partner because it would mean that he would be giving up on the idea that "I am lovable." On the surface, staying with an abusive partner seems self-destructive, but looking through the Taoist lens we discover that the logic being used by this client seems not so unreasonable. This also allows the provider to endorse a non-pathological perspective, turning "illness" into "adaptiveness." This also allows the client to re-vision other options that would also support the idea that he may indeed be lovable.

The Taoist move to convert the attribution "pathological" to "adaptive" is similar to the familiar family therapy technique of reframing. When an elementary school girl was dragged into my office with the label, "pyromaniac," and I was told by her parents that she was creating unbearable drama and chaos for her family, we quickly learned that she felt that lighting fires was the only way she was able to stop her parents from fighting and abusing each other. "I was terrified that they would get a divorce." For the Taoist therapist, it is easy to resonate with this frightened child's discovery of the power of paradox.

Eugenia Hanfmann (1978) the founder of the Brandeis University counseling center, would often declare that the job of the counselor and psychotherapist was to "find the health within the pathology." She did not identify herself as a Taoist but her thinking was exactly compatible with what I saw as Taoist theology. She would sometimes refer to the "jealous possessive" lover as someone who was communicating an inflated need and dependency in a way that could be reframed (Jujitsu) as a positive behavior or attitude. The accused partner could then develop a more compassionate reaction that would not condone the possessive behavior but would allow the victim to see this behavior through a more generous and less hostile lens.

Grace Unfolding

Embedded in my youth (yin), there was a capacity to understand those who struggled to read and to learn. As a high school senior, I harbored a fantasy of entering Boston College as an athlete and was rejected in 1966. In 1999 (yang), I was honored as one of 8 "Exemplary Professors" with more than 200 students asserting in writing on their evaluations, "Dr. King was the best professor I had at Boston College." There was more to the athlete (Yin) that developed over time such that the mind (Yang) could emerge in the balance of my journey from youth to elder.

For me, Taoism is a path and a map to spiritual, emotional physical and mental health. It is the glimmer of light at the end of the tunnel. It is a shelter from insanity and a sanctuary for spiritual growth, expansion, and rejuvenation. It is the force and the capacity to yield.

Finding an Affirming Community

Twenty five years ago, about 15 years after completing my master's degree in counseling and my doctorate in psychology, I joined a professional group of nine internationally, racially, spiritually, linguistically, and culturally diverse mental health professionals, most of them psychologists. We committed ourselves to a pursuit of cultural competence and humility. We originally described ourselves as the Boston Institute for Culturally Accountable Practices, with the intent of holding each and all of us in the group accountable for affirming cultural awareness and humility, including taking responsibility for blind spots and blunders in our relationships with each other and with others outside of our group. We have changed our name to the Boston Institute for Culturally *Affirming* Practices (BICAP, 2017). This change further endorses my Taoist orientation, in that the Tao aggressively promotes a balanced look at health and pathology and requires commitment to searching for what has been missed, hidden, or overlooked. The compatibility between this group and my Taoist theology is rich, inspirational, and empowering.

Walking in the Way of the Tao

I feel very deeply that I have an encounter with the Almighty every time I walk out into the rain, *or* walk out into the bright, and sometimes hot and humid, sun. Likewise I communicate with Her when I walk into the snow or remove the ice from my frozen windshield and experience the total darkness that is the mystery and power of the Almighty. I encounter the sacred on the many visits that I have made to the Nile River, and the weekly visits that I now make to the Mississippi River. As I witness these spectacles of unrelenting power and flexibility, I am consumed by the flow of the Tao. I embrace fear as one of the ways I connect with the Almighty. It is part of the wisdom that He has granted to me and is a profoundly useful tool for survival. The majesty of She is exquisite, intimidating, devastating, comforting, and rejuvenating. Her balance is the gospel and it is divine.

References

Boston Institute for Culturally Affirming Practices. (2017). Deconstructing power to build connection: An imperative for human services. In E. Pinderhughes, V. Jackson, & P. Romney (Eds.), *Understanding power: An imperative for human services* (pp. 195–218). Washington, DC: National Association of Social Workers Press.

Chungliang, C. A., & Lynch, J. (1999). *Tao mentoring: Cultivating collaborative relationships in all areas of your life*. New York: Marlowe and Company.

Hanfmann, E. (1978). *Effective therapy for college students*. San Francisco: Jossey-Bass.

Siegmann, J. (2000). *The Tao of tango*. Bloomington, Indiana: Trafford.

Meaning Making Through Family Constellation Work

Linda Longo-Lockspeiser

> Listen to the wind, it talks. Listen to the silence, it speaks. Listen to your heart, it knows.
> —Native American Proverb

Introduction

Family Constellations or Systemic Constellations is a phenomenological healing process that makes visible the unconscious dynamics in a family system. It uses the embodied experience of representatives for family members in a group setting which allows us to see what is out of balance, who or what is missing, and what is needed to bring the system back to harmony. It is a process that goes to the heart of the matter, to the soul's deepest yearnings and needs, and to the spiritual truth of the dilemmas we face. It is a way of healing the individual soul by aligning it in right relationship to the family soul. Using intuition and attending mindfully to the subtle somatic experience of the representatives, we tune into the heretofore unseen bonds of love that keep family members connected on a soul level.

This soul realm is distinct from both the somatic or personal realms that have traditionally been attended to by medicine or psychotherapy. We speak of the soul when we are referring to the subjective experience by which we feel emotions like yearning, compassion, despair, and hope. These experiences live in the space between body and mind. It is in this space that we find meaning and value. It has different needs from the body and a different logic from the mind, although it is not separate from either (Beaumont, 2012). In Constellation work, we attend to this soul realm of both the individual and the family.

L. Longo-Lockspeiser (✉)
Private Psychotherapy Practice, Valley Stream, NY, USA

D. Trimble (ed.), *Engaging with Spirituality in Family Therapy*, AFTA SpringerBriefs in Family Therapy, https://doi.org/10.1007/978-3-319-77410-7_7

The family soul is the energy unique to each family that holds the memory of what has happened in the family through the generations. It includes all members of the system living and dead, as well as anyone who has played an important role in the family story. So, for example, anyone who commits a crime causing death or injury to someone in the family would be connected to that family soul. So, too, are adoptive and foster parents and first loves.

While we inherit many wonderful qualities, talents, and values from our family, sharing sadness appears to keep us profoundly bonded and reinforces our sense of belonging in the system. Based on the empirical work of Bert Hellinger (1999), this method provides a living map for healing intergenerational wounds even when the details are obscured from the client. While this has been one of the more challenging aspects about Constellation work, research in the fields of epigenetics (Skinner, 2015), bonding and attachment (Hellinger et al., 1999), trauma treatment (Levine, 2015), and quantum physics (McTaggart, 2008) has begun to shed some light on how representatives can "know" information about people they never met. However, there is still much that is Mystery. Devastating patterns that plague some families through the generations such as alcoholism, violence, and depression begin to make sense when viewed from a Constellation lens. The insights gained provide new meaning to the current struggles and create the possibility for healing in cases where other traditional therapeutic methods may have been of limited consequence.

Over the last 35 years, the focus of my clinical work has evolved from symptom reduction to creating space for clients to think about what they believe about their life, its purpose, and what they want their legacy to be once they are gone. I grew up in a family where there were lots of inconsistencies between how we talked about our family and how it felt to live in my home. It inspired an early curiosity in me about the deeper meanings of life. Later in my clinical work, I began using a spiritual lens to explore the meaning clients ascribed to the persistence of their suffering as well as to its potentiality for growth and healing. Those clients with the most challenging circumstances often believed they just did not deserve a life that could engender joy, creativity, or love. Constellation work was developed originally for those clients with seemingly intractable problems. In the past 30 years, its principles and techniques have been expanded to address systemic issues in organizations and communities around the world, especially in Europe, Asia, and South America.

This chapter will illustrate the systemic thinking underpinning Constellation work. It will also describe how essential feedback from "representatives" informs the work. It will include both the author's personal journey and clinical vignettes to exemplify how uncovering and acknowledging what was lost in the family's past can return us to our rightful place in the family system. When we do so, there is a felt sense of peace and balance that is real and powerful, albeit "difficult to describe," an often heard comment. It attests to the challenge of putting words to a spiritual process, which, I believe, Constellation work is.

Origin of Constellation Work

> The peace of the dead is dependent on the living, and the wellness of the living is dependent on the dead. —Anonymous

Bert Hellinger (b.1925), who developed Constellation Work, grew up during the Third Reich in Germany. He was protected from its hateful indoctrination by the religious beliefs of his devout Catholic parents. After being drafted and subsequently captured in Belgium by the Allies, he returned home and became a Catholic priest. He was eventually sent to South Africa as a missionary where he was moved by the Zulus' respect for and connection to their ancestors through ritual and prayer. Similar to Native American spirituality, the Zulus believed that those who died continued to have an important influence on their daily life. Observing their devotion to ancestors, Hellinger came to value our interconnectivity even in death, "the communion of saints" in the Christian tradition. He remained in South Africa for almost 20 years after which he returned to his native Germany, left the priesthood, and became certified in psychoanalysis.

Hellinger quickly realized that most of the individual problems he was treating were connected to the family. He came to believe that many of the symptoms presented by patients were actually the spiritual legacy of World War II as it was uniquely passed down in each family. He observed a "frozen grief" that blocked the flow of love and life in the German culture not only because of the devastation and horror of the war but also because of a collusive silence in the families of both victims and perpetrators of Nazism. After many years addressing the terrible effects of this unacknowledged grief and trauma in his work, he developed Systemic Family Constellations, his unique contribution to the field (Hellinger et al., 1999).

Family Constellation Work integrates aspects of many philosophies, modalities, and theories about healing, in particular, Family Systems theory and the power of group. Hellinger studied Gestalt therapy, Primal therapy, and Transactional Analysis and borrowed from Satir's "Sculpting" and Moreno's "Psychodrama." However, he became more interested in what created change in the clients' felt experience than in following any particular theory for its own sake. His work draws heavily on Boszormenyi-Nagy's (1984) construct of "invisible loyalties," believing that symptoms are actually the soul's attempt to stay connected to their family system out of unconscious love and loyalty. Based on his observations, Hellinger hypothesized that symptoms, even serious symptoms such as suicide and chronic illness, were partly unconscious child-like attempts to stay connected on a spiritual level to excluded or unacknowledged members of the family system. He called this phenomenon an "entanglement" when someone blindly takes on the fate of a family member or repeats some negative pattern from their life.

Hellinger's focus was on this energetic family system or "family soul" and how individuals are impacted when they are not in right relationship in that system. His understanding of conscience, guilt, and innocence can be understood in terms of maintaining this balance in relationships. Conscience in his view is what tells the members what must be done to secure belonging to a group—thus remaining "innocent"—and what cannot be done without risking "guilt." So, for example, one may feel "innocent" and justified to commit horrendous atrocities in loyalty to one's family or country such as killing in wartime, while burning one's draft card to avoid going to an unjust war may engender "guilt." The justification for slavery in the USA and the denial of its intrinsic economic impact on white wealth until the present day is a poignant example of "innocence" in the service of blind loyalty to white ancestors who may have owned slaves and benefited from their free labor. In this way, one can justify blaming African Americans for the poverty in their devastated communities with a clear conscience.

The Constellation Method

Family Constellations were originally developed for a group setting. The client brings a problem that is usually something that has been resistant to other forms of therapy and has a sense of urgency (energy): a chronic illness, relationship or work issues, or intractable emotional and/or psychological symptoms such as anxiety or depression. There is a brief interview during which the facilitator explores what the client would like as an outcome, for example, to be able to let go of a destructive relationship or to feel more hopeful about her life. The facilitator listens for basic facts about what might be impacting the present situation. When there are no major events in the client's personal history, the facilitator looks for early deaths, losses, or traumas from previous generations that significantly impacted the course of family history. These may also typically include immigration, natural disasters, or war as well as the loss of a first love, miscarriage, abortion, or releasing a child for adoption.

From the very beginning of the interview, the facilitator is privately tracking possible themes, sometimes creating a genogram as a visual tool. However, any possible hypotheses are held lightly by the facilitator so as to remain humble and open to the movement of energy in a space of respectful unknowing. At times, the client has no conscious awareness of relevant events or does not make any useful connections, but then he remembers that there has not been contact with one side of the family for years or jokes that the family always said he reminded them of an uncle who died young! An important caveat to this work is NOT to assume uncritically that past events explain the present, as no one is immune to the vagaries of life, and most families have some traumatic events in their history. Rather, it is when an event is so shameful or overwhelming or has become a secret that it has the potential of creating a block in the flow of love in the system that can be transmitted transgenerationally through our genes or through mirroring.

Once a theme or pattern is identified, the client chooses group members as representatives for himself and relevant family members. Without much deliberation and following his intuition, the client guides the representatives to stand in spatial relationship to each other. When this living map of the conscious dynamics in the family is set up, the client sits down and watches. This provides emotional distance to observe and take in the Constellation. The representatives are instructed to tune in to their body, to forget what they heard about the story, and to objectively and without judgment or analysis report physical sensations, feelings, or movements they are experiencing. The pace is slow and quiet with little talking. What follows is an unfolding of the unspoken story of the family. The facilitator follows her intuition about what questions to ask, whom to move, or healing words ("words of empowerment") that either name "what is" or resolve what is out of balance. Seeing, acknowledging, honoring, and accepting "what is" remains key to opening the heart to let go of what was once held as truth by the client. Throughout, the facilitator tracks information from three sources: the facts of the story, the reports of the representatives, and systemic ideas or "orders of love," e.g., everyone has a place in the system and everyone has a right to belong; healthy relationships have a balance of give and take; and those who come first deserve our respect. When all the representatives find their rightful place and they feel calm, the client may come in to stand in the Constellation so as to feel the healing energy created.

This ability to intuitively know what is at least metaphorically true in Constellations by the client and later by representatives was given the term "The Knowing Field" by German psychiatrist and medical doctor Albrecht Mahr (1999). He was inspired to do so after the work of Rupert Sheldrake on "morphogenetic fields" and morphic resonance. Sheldrake observed many species of animals, especially fish or birds, and their ability to synchronize their movements in resonance with each other without any formal communication. He hypothesizes that it is an energetic blueprint stored in our DNA that contains all that has occurred in the past and present (Sheldrake, 2009). It is similar to Jung's ideas about the "Collective Unconscious" (Jung, 1968). It is in this field that Ervin Laszlo suggests that transpersonal connections independent of time and space are made from which we can draw information such as the thoughts, feelings, and sensations of the person being represented (Laszlo, 2007).

Illustration

In one Constellation, a client James (age 55) described the tense and often distant relationship he experienced with his adult son. While he loved him a great deal, he had difficulty expressing his love, often impulsively judging and criticizing him for minor offenses. Consequently, his son treated him with disdain and avoidance. He yearned for more closeness and warmth and blamed his wife for too often getting in the middle.

During the interview, I learned that James had left home just after high school. He had met his wife while he was in the service; after marrying, they settled across the country from his hometown. He reported that his relationship with his father was also cold and distant, recounting many instances of harsh criticism from him as he was growing up. He avoided visiting and spoke to his dad infrequently. He explained that his grandfather had been very abusive to his father, but that he, James, had never been physically mistreated by his grandfather.

Upon my suggestion, James chose three representatives: one for himself, one for his father, and one for his mother. He guided his "mother" to stand two feet in front of his "father" face to face, while his own representative was placed watching from a distance. The "father" reported feeling dead inside and lonely, the "mother" torn between her husband and her son. James' representative felt wary and angry. The family energy field felt stuck; no one felt an inclination to move. I asked James about his father's history, learning that he had served in the Pacific during the World War II. His father never spoke about his experience. Upon hearing this, the "father" then offered that he now felt overcome with guilt and sadness. The "mother" felt compassion for her husband but was still tentative to approach him. The representative for James reported feeling curious.

I then placed a representative for "The War" behind the "father," who immediately covered his face and began to weep silently. Everyone in the room was moved by his tears, including James' representative who took a step closer to his "parents." When asked, the "father" replied, "I am so ashamed. I'm afraid they will hate me if they knew." What seemed to be a cold and harsh man was really an emotionally wounded and traumatized old soldier who was afraid of infecting his family with the evil he had witnessed and participated in.

With that, I gave the "mother" words to say to her "husband," "You sacrificed so much for us. I didn't understand your pain. I see it now. You don't have to protect us from it any longer." There was an audible release of breath by the "father," and his stance relaxed as his "wife" moved to stand beside him as if in support. James' representative now directly facing his "father" was instructed to say, "Dear Dad, I thought you didn't love me. I felt so alone." James' representative began to tear up, as did James, when the "father" opened his arms to embrace his "son." The representative for "The War" retreated.

Within a few moments, the representative for James reported feeling as if his heart were broken open. At this point, I suggested James come into the Constellation to stand in his place, with his representative and those of his "parents" behind him. Once I saw he had taken in the energy of his "parents," I brought in the representatives for James' wife and son and directed them to find a good place. His "wife" walked to his left side and the "son" stood in front of him. A few tentative moments passed, and then James spontaneously said to him, "Now I can see you." James and his "son" smiled and hugged. When family members find their way to each other with love and respect and everyone finds his appropriate place, the Constellation ends.

My Journey to Family Constellation Work

Personal History

Like most sojourners, my spiritual path has taken a circuitous route. I am a cisgender heterosexual woman at the end of my 6th decade. I am married with four adult children and one stepdaughter. I was born the oldest of six children to Italian

American parents; three of my grandparents were immigrants. My father had to work three jobs to support us as he had left high school to support his widowed mother and his four surviving siblings. I was raised in a mostly Italian, Irish, and Jewish neighborhood where family came first, respect for elders was given, and helping care for younger siblings was second only to going to school. My father brought us to Mass every Sunday while Mom stayed home and made the gravy (aka "sauce" to non-Italians) for Sunday dinner. Sunday dinner was the highlight of the week, partly because Dad was home to eat with us and partly because it was almost always shared with extended family or friends. It was an all-day ritual filled with good food and wine, shared conversation, and opera playing in the background. We knew whom we belonged to when we prayed grace before the meal and what roles each of us held by where we sat at the table. To this day, this indelible image imprinted on my soul continues to define what "Family" is to me—connection, sharing food, and love.

Despite these warm memories, in the shadow of my soul for as long as I can remember, I worried about my parents. In fact at age ten, I was hospitalized for a week for what was diagnosed as stress related symptoms. I stayed awake late at night trying to hear my parents' conversations to make sense of what I was experiencing. I knew they loved us and each other, but my Mom was often distracted and my Dad was moody and unpredictably explosive. He could be playful and silly with us. However, when I turned six or seven that all changed. His moodiness increased, keeping us at a distance for fear of "getting in trouble." I was to learn many years later that his father had died suddenly when my Dad was seven leaving him as the functional male head of the household. I have come to appreciate how that event effectively ended my Dad's own childhood and plunged his family into poverty.

My relationship with my Mom was one of apprenticeship in caring for the younger children and in sharing her burdens. Caring for babies was like play for me and my sister, but it was my role as my Mom's comforter that was overwhelming. I became hyper-vigilant about her emotional state. I never knew exactly what triggered her emotional meltdowns, so I made sure I never gave her something to worry about with me. I learned to deal with life on my own and to put on a happy face when my Dad would send me to check that Mom was okay. This led to my later struggles and confusion around boundaries, personal limitations, and over-responsibility.

By the age of seven, I had learned well to be a "good girl" in an attempt to avoid triggering my Dad's rage and to assure my Mom that she could count on me. Before I could even name what was happening, my identity became cemented in the role of caretaker. It was only after years of working with traumatized clients that I came to understand the origin of my father's frightening outbursts as symptoms of PTSD from World War II, and my mother's depression from the loss of her firstborn child. However, it was my own Constellation work that finally opened my heart to fully accept the deep love from and connection to my father and my mother that eventually freed me to be more present to my own partner and children.

Music, Liturgy, and the Church

My formal education through college was in the Catholic school system, but what really moved my soul were the beautiful church rituals, the soaring music, and the original Latin texts that transported me to another realm. These attuned me to an easy acceptance of Mystery as an integral part of life. I found comfort and solace at church, and it gave me a safe place to let go of the over-responsibility I felt in the outside world. I loved being part of a community connected through a shared faith in a loving, merciful God, even if its representatives did not always model that. Somehow, during liturgy, my conflicted feelings about the apparently arbitrary pronouncements of the institutional church disappeared. I felt held in liminal space by something beyond my cognitive understanding. I experienced a blurring of barriers between myself and those present, and felt more loving and open hearted, especially at the Kiss of Peace, at Eucharist, and later, when I became a leader of song.

After a painful divorce in my forties that was not sanctioned by the Church, I experienced a crisis in faith that eventually forced me to let go of internalized rules from my childhood that constricted my soul. This was not an overnight process, but with the compassion of a spiritual director and the support and wisdom of the women and structure of my Twelve Step group for Relationship Addiction, I found a peace I had never enjoyed before. Richard Rohr, a Franciscan priest and visionary voice in the Catholic tradition echoes John of the Cross in describing what felt to me like a spiritual breakdown. He describes it as a "dark night of the soul" experience that nudges us to enter the darkness of the void before we can arrive at "spirituality for the second half of life" (2012). This was a space that led me to feel more expansive and more creative, where I ultimately let go of the container that formed me because I was no longer motivated by fear of "getting in trouble," but rather by a deep abiding Love.

Body, Mind, and Spirit Connection

As psychotherapists, we cannot help but come face to face with the problem of anxiety in its chronic, often debilitating, and sometimes life-threatening forms. It can hold us back from using our gifts to create a life that is fulfilling and joyful. It is a symptom of entanglement and conflict of values; it is a sign of the "guilt" Hellinger describes when one acts contrary to the unspoken family rules for belonging that we intuitively hold. I had known disabling anxiety intimately without ever giving it a name. The internal sense of deadening powerlessness was too often a familiar part of my personal landscape. Even though it numbed me in social situations, reduced me to a state of paralyzing inertia in my professional life, and glued me to unhealthy personal relationships, I believed for a long time that this was normal.

But not always… sometimes I would experience a spurt of confidence and purpose that would lower the volume on my anxiety and self-doubt. I would be inspired to begin a new project, and I could reach out with surprisingly affirming consequences. I offered to volunteer with a children's choir and became the cantor at my Church. I agreed to fill in for a supervisor at a community mental health clinic on maternity leave, and I became the clinical supervisor. I joined a peer network and was asked to give a retreat day for social workers. Even my personal life opened up, and I reconnected with a former colleague, fell in love, and eventually married my soul mate. To the outside world, I looked like an accomplished woman in her fifth decade blessed with a successful personal and professional life. And yet, there were times when all my accomplishments seemed to be a delusion, and I was brought back to that place of shame, self-doubt, and powerlessness.

Vertigo as Teacher

My journey back home to my Self began with a medical condition that had plagued me for about 15 years beginning with the birth of my second child. Disabling vertigo would occur unpredictably but usually after a particularly stressful time. The last and longest episode persisted for 2 weeks, requiring isolation in a dark and silent room. Feeling desperate and powerless to help myself, I finally surrendered to prayer. Almost instantly, the very clear awareness came flooding in that I was making myself dizzy. In attempting to fix everyone and everything around me, I was sacrificing my own health. I was humbled, and it was obvious that I had to let go of these unrealistic expectations or continue to suffer. Relaxing this over-responsibility was the beginning of releasing my need for a physical symptom that would stop me in my tracks and force me to look at my obsessive mind and inability to relax. Once I did, I never suffered from vertigo again. It was my introduction to the very real connection between body, mind, and spirit.

> *Reiki*—"Trust the energy and not to worry" (Personal communication, Reiki master Josephine Miranda).

A number of guideposts helped me find a new spiritual ground on which to rebuild my life and eventually led to Constellation work. In 1992, I was initiated into the ancient Eastern tradition of Reiki (Universal Life Force) healing modality that recognizes the interconnectivity of all energy that can be used to restore balance and harmony to body, mind, and spirit. It respects the innate wisdom of the body to draw energy to the source of the imbalance underlying symptoms. It personally released something in me and gave me courage to quit a job that I had long outgrown. I went on to open a private clinical practice where I eventually added Reiki to traditional psychotherapy for interested clients. They reported an experience of peace and serenity that was new for them and gave them the energy to participate more fully in their therapy work.

Reiki is a spiritual healing art. While my personal experience of it convinced me of its power to calm my soul, I still held some skepticism that it could help others physically. One client in particular healed my disbelief and confirmed once again that all is connected.

Illustration

Joanie was a 12-year-old girl bedridden for about 6 months by a life-threatening pulmonary problem. She literally struggled to exhale. We agreed to the protocol of four consecutive sessions of Reiki typical for chronic conditions. Joanie was a very timid child, but by the second session on the table, she began hinting that she accepted being sick. It inspired me to offer her a talk session during which she confessed that she was glad to be sick so she would not have to visit her divorced father who terrified her with his rage and inappropriate sexual behavior. Her body had offered the best solution to an impossible situation by keeping her safe in bed. That night was Joanie's first full night of sleep in months. By the fourth session, she had the courage to ask for a one-year hiatus from all contact with her father, to which he agreed. Within 2 weeks, this young girl returned to school with no physical impairment. The doctors could not explain her apparently spontaneous recovery. Her recovery was confirmation for me that something greater than me was operative and that trusting in this Presence was key to healing, even if I could not quite explain it or even discuss it with colleagues who, I feared, might judge me as unprofessional.

Constellation Work: An Invitation

Just as the body is a system with each part intricately connected to every other part, so too, is the intergenerational family system. While my postgraduate work was primarily in Bowenian family therapy, and I use genograms as an integral tool in identifying themes and patterns in families, my journey took a giant leap toward developing a cohesive integrative practice using a spiritual approach 12 years ago when I read an article entitled, "How to Heal Your Family" (Palmer, 2006). It described Family Constellation work and how seeing the hidden dynamics operating in families was the first step in healing the family. This was during a period of my life just after my father's death. We were still adjusting to the inevitable shifts that occur after losing the central figure in a family. I was acutely aware of the many faces of grief that were surfacing in our family interactions, and when I read the article, I recognized the truth of what was happening in our relationships.

Constellations seemed to be a culmination of all I had learned about families, suffering, somatic memory, mindfulness, intuition, and intergenerational trauma. The organizing systemic principles were familiar to me, but making the shift from cognitive insight to the healing of the heart still eluded me too often. I made a commitment to learn how and why Constellation work appeared to be such a powerful tool, but before I could research it further, I received an email invitation to a workshop being given by a facilitator quoted in the article. Since I did not know the writer, it felt like validation to explore this mysterious process.

First Constellation Workshop

I decided to follow my intuition and attend my first workshop. I was chosen as a representative in the first Constellation of a young woman whose creative work had stagnated. She was hoping for some release from whatever internal barriers were holding her back. I was asked to represent her mother. She placed me at a distance from the representatives for herself, her husband, and her two children. We were directed to simply follow any internal movements and to move as requested when asked. Immediately upon entering the circle, strong emotions and sensations surfaced in me that were not my own. It was as if I were channeling the person I represented, even though I was given very little information beyond my relationship as the client's mother. I felt paralyzed with despair and unable to engage with the representative for the client/my "daughter" despite her attempts to engage me. I felt disconnected, surrounded by an impenetrable, invisible wall. It was only after a representative for my "mother" (the client's "grandmother") was brought in to stand behind me that I became emotionally reactive, first with fear and trepidation of her criticism, then with relief and childlike tears when she seemed to soften towards me. "I blamed you," she said to me. The facilitator looked for verification from the client who explained that her grandmother had become embittered after her grandfather had left home one night and never returned. The grandmother's representative softened once her own hurt and sadness were acknowledged. Now, when she looked at me with tears in her eyes instead of anger and rejection, I felt deep relief and energy washing over me.

When these emotions in me settled, I was turned to face the representative for my daughter, "the client." My previously frozen heart was brimming with love and acceptance. This time, when she approached me, I could take her into my arms, and she wept with joy. As often happens, there was a parallel reaction with the client watching the process. She reported an almost indescribably deep sense of peace and love.

This first Constellation convinced me that something profound had occurred on a number of levels. I felt a deep resonance with the client, as did many of the witnesses. Like the client, I, too, had been feeling stuck in my creative life. My fear of failure and criticism was paralyzing at times. Somehow, after the Constellation, I felt a calming sense of peace and harmony. Subsequent to this Constellation, I returned to voice lessons, after having left singing behind years before for reasons that I was to learn later in my own Constellation work.

Intergenerational Loss in My Family of Origin

Merging With My Mother

There are many losses and secrets I have discovered over the last 10 years of working with Constellations that had affected my life in invisible ways. One had to do with my becoming pregnant at the age of 19. After informing my parents of my pregnancy, I learned that my mother had also delivered a baby who was secretly released for adoption. She had been studying at Juilliard and performing with an opera company on tour at the time of her pregnancy. She was 19. I kept my child and juggled college, childcare, and a difficult marriage, but my mother and I never spoke about our shared experience again, remaining loyal to the family rule about never talking about "the secret we both knew."

Many years later, an appreciation for the profound systemic consequences of that secret became more apparent in a Constellation I attended to seek some insight around a pattern of starting and stopping in my professional life. Tremendous anxiety had surfaced again as I began preparing for a singing engagement. What emerged from the feedback of the representatives during a Constellation was how depressed and anxious my mother was in relation to her firstborn. The decision to release this child for adoption was not her own; rather, it was my grandmother's, whose representative sadly explained, "I thought I was protecting her." It was clear from the representative for my mother that some part of her spirit had shut down in being forced to give her child away. She never sang professionally again nor did she ever complete college. My chronic anxiety and intermittent depression now made sense in light of these new images. A child's blind love knows no bounds. The worst pain is to see a parent suffering. What released me from carrying my mother's pain were the words that emerged from that Constellation session, "Out of love and loyalty, I suffer like you, Mom." In contrast to unconscious loyalty, conscious love acknowledges the sacrifices and sufferings but chooses life in honor of that person.

Identifying With My Grandfather

My mother once remarked that I got the best and the worst of both sides of the family. Indeed, there does seem to be a pattern that the eldest child becomes entangled with unfinished business from both sides of the family tree. Beyond the story of my mother and her interrupted life path, there is the story of my paternal grandfather, who was not only a Catholic priest in Italy but also a musician until he left the priesthood and immigrated to the USA. I only learned this a few years before my father's death. Looking back, I realize that it was not a coincidence that my father, not my mother, was the parent who encouraged me to study music. Mom had too much unresolved trauma from that chapter of her life to be supportive. It is also no wonder to me today why I suffered so much internal conflict whenever I performed. I know now that I carried not only my parents' losses but my grandfather's, as well, whose musical gifts were lost and forgotten in his immigration story.

Personal Impact of Constellation Work

Opening My Heart to My Mother

Through my work with Constellations, I have made peace with the many conflicting energies that have impacted my life. In seeing the connection between my mother's depression and the early loss of her first child, I was able to connect with her in a much more compassionate way. My heart opened to my mother's pain, sacrifice, and most importantly, her courage. The arrogant position I took in my heart that made me think I knew better what was good for her softened, and I stopped trying to suggest ways she could feel better. This shifted my place in relation to my Mom from one of peer or even parent to my rightful place as her child. There was more ease in our interactions and, for the first time in my life, I was able to ask for her comfort when I was going through a crisis. It seemed to lift her spirit to know that she had contributed to my life in an important way. When I told her how much I appreciated and needed her, she replied, "Wonderful, that's all I need to know." At the time, I thought it a bit odd, but in retrospect, I realized that a mother's role is to give and a child's to receive. Because of the consequences of her unacknowledged losses and secrets, I had learned to give but not to receive, thus robbing my mother of the opportunity to mother me.

Becoming One of the Gang

Another important shift in my "place" in the family was in relation to the birth order of my older unknown sibling. Following my first personal Constellation, I had an insight about my ambivalence and insecurity being in leadership positions. The internal voice I had often struggled to silence was, "Who do you think you are?" This sense of not being enough had resulted in vertigo years before. Now, it was tied to disabling doubts around the issue of authority in every area of my life. What surfaced in the Constellation was the awareness that I was not, indeed, the eldest child of my mother. I became aware that the internal pressure to be over-responsible was at least partly connected to an unconscious need to make up for a sibling who was invisible except in my soul. No wonder that I could never feel that I was enough! On a soul level, I could never take my older sister's place.

Once I saw this in the Constellation and humbly acknowledged my sister in my heart, I felt a different kind of peace. The impact on my relationships was dramatic. I was finally in my right relationship not only to my other siblings but with friends and colleagues, as well. I could more easily ask for and accept help without shame, I let go of the need to be perfect and to know everything (as if this were ever possible!), and I could finally enjoy my siblings as peers. I learned to relax and to listen. I got more humble. I was finally in my right place in the family.

Reclaiming Our Legacy of Music

There was one more lasting shift that was around my relationship with music and the Church. My feelings about the Church had always been conflicted. As explained earlier, I loved liturgy and the music that accompanied it. I had cantored in Church for many years and given it up for reasons that I thought were about politics in my parish. What I have come to know in my heart is that my leaving had more to do with loyalty to my paternal grandfather. He had also become disillusioned with the Church and lost everything in leaving the priesthood—including his family, status, and financial stability. When he died after only 10 years in this country, he was denied burial from the Church because of the family's inability to make the required donation. In acknowledging "what was," I was able to let go of the unconscious "guilt" about being an integral part of parish events, and I have returned to liturgical music with a joyful heart that honors my grandfather and what he left behind.

This legacy of music has also been passed down to my children, and it continues to inspire and energize our family. My two oldest participate in a number of oratorio societies and chorales. One daughter helped start a new orchestra with a colleague, and she is coming up on her twentieth anniversary as a director at Juilliard—the school my mother never graduated from. My son joined the same opera company that, unbeknownst to any of us, my mother had sung with over 70 years before, where she had been a lead in *La Boheme*. We accompanied my mother to my son's first performance with this company, which, coincidentally was *La Boheme.* It is a memory we will always cherish. He had dedicated the performance to his grandmother in the program notes, and the director acknowledged her from the stage after the performance. That was 3 years before she died. When my Mom passed 2 years ago, the family "choir" of about thirty all sang her favorite hymn at her funeral mass, the prayer of St. Francis of Assisi, "Make Me a Channel of Your Peace," a treasured postscript to a poignant chapter of her life and legacy.

Finally, my Dad, who never had the opportunity to study music but was always so proud of my Mom's voice, had been deprived of any acknowledgement or appreciation for his role in passing on a love of music to us, especially opera. After his death and upon my daughter's suggestion, we instituted a vocal scholarship for an opera major at Juilliard in my parents' names that will continue in perpetuity. In addition, we continue the family tradition of song each year we meet for Christmas Carols or for our latest venture, singing through the scores of beloved Broadway shows. The family soul is finally at peace and in harmony!

Alternative Settings for Constellation Work

Traditionally, Constellations are facilitated in a group setting where the participants may come to act as observers who hold the Knowing Field, as representatives, or as seekers/clients to do their own work. The workshop usually begins with a brief orientation with particular attention to the goal of being of service to each other in a safe, nonjudgmental space. They are reminded that this is an intuitive process and that there are no mistakes possible. Everything has its place in the system. They are encouraged to be mindful to the subtlest shifts in their somatic experience and to avoid analyzing.

I have also found that they can have just as powerful an impact in individual, couple, and family settings. Because of the more intimate setting of the therapy office, clients who are somewhat hesitant about a group experiential process are more likely to agree to one here. I use small figures for tabletop Constellations, or papers or floor markers when I want the client to actually stand in a particular role. Imaginal Constellations with closed eyes are also useful for those who are more reserved about expressing feelings. Having a parent stand on a floor marker as a representative for their irascible child or disrespectful adolescent often helps the parent appreciate their child's confusion and anxiety, thus increasing empathy and hope and sidestepping the typical parent worry about shame and blame.

Constellations in supervision and consultations can be a short cut to getting to the "heart of the matter" when colleagues have reached a stalemate in treatment. In supervision, it is helpful to set up representatives for both the client and his/her family of origin and the therapist and his/her family of origin. In these Constellations, the therapist is often able to see patterns from his family of origin that may be creating a block in the therapeutic process. In a consultation at a children's psychiatric hospital, a brief Constellation helped identify the source of "resistance" in the mothers' support group. What surfaced was the mothers' shame over being judged by the mostly unmarried treatment team and their fear about expressing it directly. Once the staff experienced the mothers' shame in the Constellation, they were moved to work harder to create a more respectful collaboration with the mothers in the group. Not surprisingly, the children began to improve as they were released from the loyalty bind between their family and the staff.

Illustration 1: Ripple Effect of an Early Death of a Sibling on a Marriage

The following case from my clinical practice illustrates how a short Constellation can get to the real spiritual source of the problem and open the door for more empathic connection between a couple, even when one is a reluctant participant.

Mary and Robert are Jamaican American in their early 1940s. They came in with complaints of growing distance between them emotionally and physically. They both declared their love for each other but often found themselves in drawn out arguments around Mary's feeling controlled and criticized and Robert's feeling left out of Mary's life. After spending some time getting more details about their conflict, I explained the exercise that would help me get a better picture of what they were experiencing. I brought out little figures for each of them, in turn, to set up on the table in a configuration that described how they experienced their relationship. Mary went first and set her figure at a slight angle away from her husband's figure. His figure was facing her at a close distance. I then asked about their observations and their internal experience. Mary described feeling anxious and overwhelmed, with heaviness in her shoulders and a desire to move away from Robert's figure. Joe described feeling sad and helpless, although he also admitted that his figure seemed intimidating.

When Joe set up his internal picture of their relationship, he placed Mary's figure farther away from his, and raised the arms of his figure out toward Mary's. He observed feeling an even heavier sense of powerlessness and fear that he described as tightness in his throat and head. Pointing to the Constellation, he said, "It feels like I'm losing her." Because Mary's figure seemed to be looking away somewhat, I placed a figure in the space directly in front of her gaze. She looked up curiously and asked who that could be. I was not sure, but it seemed to me that something was distracting her from facing Robert. I asked about any abortions or miscarriages, first loves, early losses in her family of origin, or other traumas in her history. She inhaled audibly, looked at Robert cautiously, and reported that her mother had lost a baby when Mary was about 8 years old. It was never talked about, of course, but Mary, typical for her age, believed she was responsible for her mother's losing the baby and her parents' subsequent divorce.

I invited her to close her eyes and to imagine this sister at whatever age she felt was right. I instructed her to repeat words I would give her unless they did not feel right for whatever reason. With her eyes closed and imagining holding her infant baby sister while looking deeply into her eyes, she repeated my words, "You are my baby sister. I love you so much. I lived and you died." Mary began to weep as the little 8-year-old released long suppressed guilt and grief. Joe gently took her hand in his. Sobbing, she cried, "I was so lonely." I reframed this to include the relational problem they had come in with. "When you died, a piece of me died, too. I kept you close by keeping out everyone else I loved." A quiet nod of affirmation confirmed Joe's experience of their relationship, and I encouraged him to move closer to her. Mary released a deep sigh of relief. While she was drained from crying, she reported also feeling somehow calm and peaceful. She was grateful for Robert's quiet presence. Robert reported feeling deeply moved and more connected to Mary than he had been in a long time. While he could not exactly say what changed for him, he now moved his figure closer to Mary's. Mary exclaimed that she had wanted to do the same thing.

Illustration 2: What Is the Soul Trying to Manifest, Resolve, or Balance?: Adolescent Girl With Obsessive Compulsive Symptoms

This case exemplifies how emotional and behavioral complaints may have their origin in a secret in the family and how bringing the secret to light can release the symptoms.

Janet was 17 when she sought treatment for a severe obsessive fear that her boyfriend was cheating on her. She could not concentrate and had difficulty sleeping. She would force herself to throw up to keep thin and would stalk her boyfriend when he was not with her. No amount of reassurance helped alleviate her symptoms. She was losing weight and despite being an A student, her marks were steadily dropping. We did a tabletop Constellation, using figures for herself, her mother, and her father. When we looked at the external picture of her internal sense of the relationships, she observed that both parents were looking away. She reported feeling anxious and frightened. Only when I spoke to her mother privately did her symptoms make sense. I learned that her parents had started their relationship as an affair and had never revealed this secret to her. Everyone else knew including her four older stepsiblings on both sides of the family. The order of precedence had not been respected. The first spouses who were left were not given a respectful place in the system. This created a great deal of conflict and tension for the other children. Janet apparently became entangled in this unfinished business and unconsciously identified with the abandoned spouses around their right to honesty and respect for their sacrifice. "Because they lost, the new couple gained." Once the secret was revealed, her obsessive fears disappeared.

Efficacy of Constellation Work: Healing the Heart

Constellation work values both the rational mind and the intuitive mind, but it particularly highlights the heart-centered consciousness of intuition. It is a wonderful tool that externalizes the problem, provides alternate perspectives, reduces shame and blame, and nurtures empathy, hope, and connection. It reconnects the individual soul to his family soul and reframes our struggles as being in loving service to forgotten members of our family. Sometimes, it even provides a realignment of the system that then restores harmony among family members who are not part of the session.

Personally, I have used this method when I feel stuck or when I have to make an important decision. I have participated in hundreds of Constellations and trainings both here and abroad. I am still awed by the power of this method to heal the heart, even as a small part of me wants to dismiss it as hocus pocus. There has been some research about its long-term efficacy, but more needs to be done in this area. Despite this limitation, Constellation work continues to inform and inspire me in both my personal and professional life. It has confirmed my deep faith in a Great Mystery that we are all a part of, a Loving Consciousness that envelops and enfolds us and from which we can draw information, guidance, and support even in the most desperate situations. Finally, this work has confirmed for me that what we often reject in our life actually holds the key to our redemption—there is a gift in the "Dark Box" (Oliver, 2006, p. 52).

> Someone I loved once gave me a *box* full of *darkness*.
>
> It took me years to understand that this too, was a gift.

References

Beaumont, H. (2012). *Toward a spiritual psychotherapy, soul as a dimension of experience*. Berkeley, CA: North Atlantic Books.

Boszormenyi-Nagy, I., & Spark, G. (1984). *Invisible loyalties: Reciprocity in intergenerational family therapy*. New York: Brunner Mazel.

Hellinger, B., Weber, G., & Beaumont, H. (1999). *Love's hidden symmetry: What makes love work in relationships*. Phoenix, AZ: Zeig, Tucker & Theisen.

Jung, C. (1968). *Collected works of C. G. jung* (Vol. 9, Part 1, 2nd ed., pp. 42–53). Princeton, NJ: Princeton University Press.

Laszlo, E. (2007). *Science and the Akashic field: An integral theory of everything* (p. 5). New York: Simon and Schuster.

Levine, P. (2015). *Trauma and memory: body and brain in a search for the living past: a practical guide for understanding and working with traumatic memory*. Berkeley, CA: North Atlantic Books.

Mahr, A. (1999). The knowing field: Family constellations as mental and energetic healing. In *Intellectual cures for a new time*. Heidelberg, Germany: Kösel Verlag.

McTaggart, L. (2008). *The field: The quest for the secret force of the universe*. New York: Harper.

Oliver, M. (2006). *"The uses of sorrow", Thirst* (p. 52). Boston, MA: Beacon Press.

Palmer, L. D. (2006, November/December). How to heal your family. *Spirituality and Health*, 50–55.

Rohr, R. (2012). *Falling upward—A spirituality for the two halves of life*. San Francisco: Jossey Bass.

Sheldrake, R. (2009). *Morphic resonance: The cause of formative causation* (p. 3). Rochester, VT: Park Street Press.

Skinner, M. (2015). Ancestral ghosts in your genome. *Ted Talk*. Retrieved from https://www.youtube.com/watch?v=f1Pf5S8Nbfk

Vision Quest: The Intersection of Native American Spirituality and Family Therapy

Rockey Robbins

This chapter offers a description of a Native American vision quest and provides suggestions about how family therapists might support clients who may have had such an experience. It challenges readers to consider the unique insights of Native American culture in the area of spiritual development. It offers a glimpse into a much maligned, persecuted, and ignored spiritual/psychological ritual path of health and healing. Family therapists would do well to consider that for traditional Native Americans, indigenous traditions for healing must always come first and that Western Psychological approaches should be supplementary. At the end of this paper, family constellations, community involvement, spiritual crisis, specific types of questioning, and cultural identity themes for therapy are considered.

More specifically, the following narrative describes a vision quest, a spiritual experience, which I partook in about 15 years ago. I had lived a life in both Native American and the White worlds. I had had many spiritual experiences during Native American dances, chanting, purification ceremonies, and peyote ceremonies. When I went to college, I began to read theology and religious literature from which I borrowed terminology to interpret my spiritual experiences. While the Western concepts were never fully adequate, they did help me to use words to at least understand them partially, and they enabled me to talk to people of other religious perspectives who had had similar experiences. I am convinced that only by sharing some of our unique cultural capital are we able to come to know and respect each other. Nonetheless, I have always been careful to limit my descriptions of my Native American spiritual experiences because as other religious groups attest, when we share too much of the esoteric of our traditions, the sacredness of the rituals may be profaned to such an extent that they become commonplace and consequently lose

R. Robbins (✉)
Department of Educational Psychology (Counseling), University of Oklahoma, Norman, OK, USA
e-mail: rockey@ou.edu

D. Trimble (ed.), *Engaging with Spirituality in Family Therapy*, AFTA SpringerBriefs in Family Therapy, https://doi.org/10.1007/978-3-319-77410-7_8

their sacred character. For the most part, what I share here are the psychological dimensions of my experience that occurred within Native American structures. I attempt to share some of the knowledge of our tribal/cultural ritual to allow readers to connect with us but not so much to lose beautiful, secret, esoteric aspects that give us our unique experiences.

A Native American vision quest (the Lakota call it *hanblechia*) entails spending time alone, usually on a remote hill, seeking visions that will guide one in one's future. Each tribe conducts the vision quest ritual differently. My vision quest was guided by a sweat lodge and Sundance group of Lakota, Cheyenne, Cherokee, and Choctaw people. Each summer, tribal Sundancers gather in groups at designated sites to dance for 4 days under the hot sun. Sweat ceremonies and vision quests are often conducted in preparation for the annual Sundances. While my group's primary approaches to sweating and conducting a vision quest were Lakota, they welcomed elements of Choctaw and Cherokee ways. For instance, Choctaw and Cherokee songs were sometimes sung in the sweat lodge, a construction consisting of a frame made of willow branches covered with tarps and blankets where water is poured over hot rocks as participants pray and sing during the sweat or purification ceremony.

Let me contextualize in theory the following account of my uncanny experience. In Lame Deer's (1972) widely recognized description, vision quests entail seeking visions and power to guide and help questers in life. The quester's blanket and pipe, filled with tobacco, provide companionship, protection, and a connection with previous generations. Not merely physical objects, they are part of Spirit, the vitality that imbues every living thing. One whose religion is limited to believing dogma and doctrine and hearing preachers is gravely mistaken to think that he or she can have a vision. To have a vision, one must know that Spirit is everywhere and is communicating to us all the time through inanimate objects, insects, animals, and so on. Lame Deer wrote of spirits of unknown origins who speak with him. He specifically mentioned fear as an emotion that he had to deal with on a deep level while on his vision quest. He explained the importance of support from the persons belonging to his lodge and especially his grandmother in his endeavor. Everyone involved believes that without having a vision the quester will be directionless.

Let me juxtapose Lame Deer's account with the ideas of Western thinkers Carl Jung (1961/1983), Rudolf Otto (1958), and William James (1902/1982), which may help non-tribal people understand the following narrative of my vision quest. Jung wrote, "The symbol is not a sign that veils something everybody knows.... On the contrary, it is an attempt to elucidate, by means of analogy something that still belongs to a domain of the unknown or something yet to be known" (p. 287). Instead of the symbol and/or dream that veils a wish or anxiety or an eruption of something repressed from the past that Freud proposed, Jung added a teleological lens onto symbols in dreams and visions, as representing something that pulls one toward self-actualization. He also added a transcendental element, suggesting that some symbols may be associated with something larger than our individual selves. Jung's perspective resonates both with Lame Deer's vision and with the one I will recount.

One of the most revered theologians of the twentieth century, Rudolf Otto, enumerated a concept of "mysterious tremendum" that is directly related to my vision quest. Mysterious tremendum refers to experiences that are beyond ordinary understanding or explanation. They always entail tremor or fear, but not fear proper. It is a primal fear that is closer to "feeling eerie and uncanny dread" (Otto, 1958, p. 14). He linked it with experiencing something that is not part of everyday ordinary experience. He argued that it has been these spiritual experiences that have prompted myths, symbols, and rituals (p. 64). William James argued that it is not the moral and ethical that is the foundation of the religious experience but the uncanny, unintelligible, wonderful experiences that have perpetuated ongoing religious expression century after century (James, 1982). Many Native American people believe that these types of experiences are invaluable, and continue to utilize rituals to incite heightened awareness. Although the rituals have solitariness as a vital element of the experiences, they are often conducted in the context of family and community.

According to Hill and Pargament (2003), rituals can trigger emotions that strengthen psychological and physiological health and healing. I knew that planning and reasoning about my spiritual predicament could not help me with my emotional and spiritual confusion. Only ritual and symbolism had provided me with the spiritual awareness to move through difficult times in my life. Up until the crisis I had before the vision quest I am about to describe, I had relied on sweat ceremonies and the Native American Church (Peyote Church). Still, I yearned for something more. I felt an emptiness, and needed direction to help me move more in a direction that would lead to greater contentment in my daily life. I realized that my life in general as a professor had congealed into a planned and controlled life that inhibited my spontaneity and connections to the immediate surround.

From the many details that I remember of my first vision quest, I extract here the merest skeleton of a series of events that appear as most important in my own and my family's current spiritual life. My hope is, that as readers read the events I describe, they will have flashes of their own memories, and in recalling them, they will be able to make connections with spiritual movements in their lives. In recalling the succession of challenging apparitional events in which I was immersed at the time, I was able to identify patterns and themes I had heretofore not recognized.

I had already attended a couple of hundred sweats at various lodges across Oklahoma. In this particular sweat lodge group, I was usually asked to lead one or two songs and had carried the rocks into the lodge a couple of times, but mostly I simply sweat and brought food for the feasts that followed. Each year, in early June, the 12–25 persons who sweat every 2 weeks at this lodge would have a person or two "put on the hill" for a vision quest. I was happy to attend each vision quest as a "supporter."

One summer evening after a sweat ceremony, I was unexpectedly gifted a pipe. The stone from which it was carved came from Pipestone, Minnesota, and the stem was made out of ash wood. Taking the pipe, I knew I was assuming great responsibility. I was to pray with it regularly, keep it clean, and handle it properly (always holding the stone in my left hand which is closest to my heart). It was suggested that I keep liquor out of my house and that I was to lead a good and pure life.

Soon after I took the pipe, I began to have dreams of "going on the hill." I dreamed I was at a school I attended as a child. Several children and I were on a small mound in the back of the country schoolhouse. We were playing "king of the hill," pushing each other off the hill. As soon as I pushed one child down the hill someone would push me, and I would find myself rolling down the hill. Ultimately, when I climbed back to the top, I found myself alone. I sat down cross-legged and looked up into the sky where I saw a hawk circling. I awoke with an inexpressible yearning for a connection to the inner unseen world. I wanted to know the deeper meaning of my life and the obstacles that kept me from evolving as a human being. I considered how I was a professor at a major university and was recognized as being knowledgeable, but lacked the wisdom to know a meaning that would give my life substance and spiritual direction. I talked with my wife and son about the dream and prayed with my pipe about what I should do.

I brought my pipe to Wiley Coyote, who ran our sweat lodge, and offered him my pipe four times. The fourth time he received it and said he would support me on a vision quest. It would begin with preparations on a morning, a sweat on that afternoon and I would be put "on the hill" late on that afternoon. I would stay "out" through two nights and a morning and be brought back to a sweat ceremony about noon. He gave me instructions to: obtain a bucket, a hatchet, a knife, and a blanket, to take with me on the vision quest, tie onto one string, 100 black, 100 red, 100 white, and 100 yellow, three green and two blue tobacco ties (small pouches of cloth containing tobacco). I was to put a prayer into every tobacco tie. I was to make four flags with tobacco offerings, the appropriate colors for each direction. I was also to make a *walutka* (Lakota name for a red square cloth with a conch shell sewed into the center and four tobacco bundles in the four corners of the cloth, which acts as an object on which to meditate while on the quest).

I talked with several people whom I trusted about the vision quest and received what I thought was valuable advice. My extended family had little to say. My father was the person who I spoke to most about it. Though he did not "sweat" or participate in vision quests himself, he was supportive. He accepted that both Choctaw and Cherokee tribal people had practiced these ceremonies, which were originally the ceremonies of different Nations, but because he had become a Christian he was "careful not to mix the spiritual ways because it was "dangerous." He was proud of me for practicing "Indian ways." But he was afraid of them himself. Talking to me in his beaded Cherokee baseball hat, he told me that an "Indian friend of his had died of bad circumstances." He added that they were often around Indians who practiced bad medicine. He told me that he often worried about me being in dangerous situations and that the vision quest was especially dangerous because I would draw both bad and good spirits. He told me that he would support me with prayers. I asked him for the hundredth time if he really cared that I practiced "Indian ways." He said he was happy that I did. When I asked why, he said, "For selfish reasons. I will be able to come to you after I die and you will know I am here. I will come to the lodge and talk to you. Christians don't really believe that." He also told me that it was better to not talk to him about it when my mother was nearby. He explained what I already knew—that she did not feel I treasured her White heritage as much as I did Dad's Indian one.

During the months leading up to the vision quest, for about an hour on a daily basis I held my pipe and prayed for others, nature, and about local and world situations and sang Native American songs, mostly Cherokee and Choctaw but also Lakota that I had learned from people who participated in our lodge. I also attended every sweat lodge ceremony we had, which were conducted regularly every other Saturday evening. Every sweat lodge gathering involved prayers for the success of the vision quest for the three of us who were being sent.

In February, I began work on my string of 405 tobacco pouches. I always began by praying with my pipe to the seven directions. Each day, I sat my pipe next to me, laid out five 2 in. square pieces of cloth, put tobacco in one after the other, praying a prayer for someone I knew. I prayed for their successful individual journeys and for their connections to their families, tribe, and others. One after the other, I tied the pouches onto a long string. I always faced the appropriate direction for prayer.

For the first 400 prayers, I envisioned all sorts of people, many whom I had forgotten long ago, arising in my mind. To my surprise, never once did I have to make an effort to conjure anyone up to pray for. I thanked each person for the time and experience they had given me. Then, I quite easily recalled a struggle they had in their lives, which came automatically. A little boy in the first grade showed himself. I remember telling my mother that I loved him because he was so sweet and he had such a country accent. He often wore a red cowboy shirt. He was physically small and weak and was pushed around and looked at the bullies with terrified eyes. He never fought back. I thanked him for the deep sensitivity he demonstrated and prayed that he learned a healthy way to deal with bullies. I saw a boss I had worked with who always thought someone was talking about her behind her back and stealing from her. I also remembered how profound her feelings seemed to be for the welfare of Native American people. I thanked her for helping me develop an even more profound heartfelt connection to tribal people, and I prayed that she would learn to trust the kind people she worked with more and thereby enjoy her life more. Close to the end of making the prayer ties, I thought of my mother. I thanked her for making our Christmases so wonderful with her cooking and her gifts and for supporting me when I chose the life journey of a scholar, which led far away from home. I prayed that we both might connect on a human level that transcended disagreements about religion and cultural lifestyle.

I knew I was learning a great deal praying for an hour each day. It was as though *Unelanvhi* (Cherokee for God) would not let me think self-interestedly. I found myself able to love every person who came to mind truly without judging them. I knew that every person I had ever met was my loving teacher, even if they hated me. I knew without a doubt that we were all helping each other to grow more aware of ourselves as being parts of something more loving and larger than we could imagine.

Summer came early. Temperatures were hitting near 100 °F, and June had not yet arrived. I remember as we were walking down a hot sidewalk in town, my wife told me to be sure to get in a shade. She did not have to say she was talking about the upcoming vision quest. I loved her so much for her concern. A week before the event, my son went with me to help chop the wood for the sweat and the fire that could not go out while I was on our hills. I remember a rattlesnake crossed the path in front of my son, a Lakota man, and me. The Lakota man said it might be a bad omen. My son quickly looked at me and said, "Not for Choctaws, huh, Dad. They are our most sacred animal. It's going to go well. The spirits are with you." I appreciated his words. Later as we stacked the wood, my son and I began to rush to complete a rick. A Cherokee man said, without looking at us, "Be gentle with these logs. Lay them down easy just as you would grandfather rocks. They are sacred." I thought, thanks for reminding me that everything is holy.

The day before our vision quest, my wife had begun to gather all the things she would need to support me. She had all the ingredients she would need to make fry bread. She and my son had laid out all the parts of the tent they would need for the encampment. They both had their wooden boxes filled with their pipes and tobacco put out on the coffee table. Occasionally, each of them would ask me how I was feeling, but the closer the event came they gave me more and more space.

The day of the vision quest arrived and I had already gone a day and a night without eating or drinking. I told Wiley Coyote and he sternly told me that I should not have done that. He explained that while this ceremony was highly communal, my experience would be solitary. No one would be with me when I was experiencing the extra anguish I would experience because of the extra sacrifice. At about 11 a.m., he told me to get my hatchet and knife. He brought me to an expansive cherry patch and advised me to find four cherry trees about 5 or 6 feet tall and to offer tobacco to earth before cutting them down. Then, I was to bring them back to his pick-up truck. It was swelteringly hot and I quickly became soaked in sweat. After I put them in the pick-up bed, he told me to find a five- or six-foot tall cedar tree and to do the same. He offered me some medicine tea when I came back to the truck but I shook my head. When we returned to the lodge, he and I built the fire in the traditional way we had been taught. The other two questers would not arrive until time to sweat. They had gone through several vision quests before and had their own unique ways of doing it. He told me that I was not to sleep and to never under any circumstances put my pipe down. I replied that I might have to use the bathroom and he said, "You won't need to. You are already depleted of water and food." He told me not to look at or speak to anyone from that moment until the vision quest was over. He had me sit about 30 yards north of the lodge.

I was brought into the lodge and seated across the dug-out hole, facing West. After preliminary remarks, Wiley Coyote asked my son, the rock carrier, to bring in seven stones to create the world. He picked out each rock carefully and with tenderness put them into his pitchfork and slid them into the lodge where they were placed in the sacred directions. The smell of sage and cedar filled the space, participants wiping their bodies with sage and a person tossing cedar on the red-hot stones. Soon, Wiley Coyote told my son to close the flap, then immediately offered a formal prayer, at first in Lakota and then in English, for all living things, including four-legged and winged ones. We all sang along to the songs we had sang in the lodge together one hundred times before, calling in the thunder beings and other spirits.

After four songs, Wiley Coyote called out to open the flap on the west side. A breeze broke through the haze and we were refreshed.

The second round was extraordinarily hot. One of the seven new rocks brought in was the largest I had ever seen in a sweat ceremony. As the pourer flung the water on the rocks, the steam splashed onto and burned our faces. Many prayers were offered during the second round and Wiley Coyote asked me explain why I had chosen to "go on an *Hanblechia.*" I told them that I had found myself in a spiritual crisis that had manifested in several areas of my life. First and foremost I felt that my inner spiritual life had been neglected leaving me spiritually directionless. I wanted help to deal with my inner turmoil and feelings of meaninglessness.

At the end of the second round, everyone except me crawled out clockwise out of the lodge. Then, I was taken out of the lodge and wrapped in a Pendleton blanket. Even my face was covered. Wiley Coyote took my arm and led me into the darkness. All those who were supporting me followed, carrying the cherry trees, cedar tree, my bucket, and its contents and my prayer ties, flags, and *walutka*. As we walked, I smelled the cedar bucket carried by my son and heard the 25 or so supporters walking through the leaves and broken branches of the densely wooded area. On the way to "my place," Wiley Coyote, stopped me four times, turning me all the way round to pray toward each direction. The last part of the walk was more of a blind climb. My feet slipped several times but Wiley Coyote caught me each time and pushed me up the hill.

Once in my place, I heard digging all around me until each of the sacrificed trees was planted around me. Then, I could hear supporters tying the direction flags on each tree and then walking the prayer ties around and around the outside of the trees. I knew I was inside a circle of prayer ties about 5½ feet in diameter. Next, a few participants chose to walk up to just outside the prayer circle and give me words of encouragement or prayers. I appreciated every person's comments, but, for the life of me, I could not recognize their voices, which at first distracted me from thinking about the content of what they were saying. Eventually, I found myself simply letting go of my need to know. I was eventually able to simply enjoy the sounds of their voices and receive their kind words. The last person who spoke to me was my wife. She is very tender-hearted and after telling me that she would be praying for my protection, she started to cry. I heard Wiley Coyote take her away whispering sweetly, "No, no, no." Lastly, the supporters sang Choctaw and Cherokee songs for me. I loved them dearly for it. They were such a wise and accepting group. Everything about the lodge was Lakota; even the other Cherokee man had "gone Lakota." But, they had always given me a little space for my tribal ways. As they sang the last song, a Cherokee one, I heard them leaving, not to return for me for 2 days.

I pulled off my blanket and spread it out below me. It was probably about an hour before sundown. I sat down in the middle of my prayer circle. I was alone. There was an elm tree to the North on my left. I could tell it probably would give me little if any shade. It had been 97 °F at 2 o'clock that afternoon. It was still probably that hot now. Already I was dehydrated. Having surveyed my situation, I felt my pipe in my hand and I was comforted. In fact, I was content, secure, and hopeful. I heard a voice in my head that told me to quit thinking and simply be where I was and to be present.

Soon after dark, tree frogs began croaking. At first, only a few sang. I was entranced. But, I began to think of them doing a symphony. I noticed the silent pauses. Then, there were so many singing, there were no pauses. Gradually, I think I began to hear them for what they were, frogs croaking, or maybe just as rhythmic sonorous noises in the night. I was wafted away. I lost track of time. When I became self-conscious again, I remember thinking, "those were not frogs croaking, that noise was all that I was. I became that noise. It was all there was in my awareness for an unknown amount of time." Again my mind took over, and I began to ruminate about time and identity. Then, I worked at trying to quit ruminating about it.

Late in the night, while my mind was jumping from one thing to the next, I heard a yelp of a coyote. Then, quickly the yelps of a whole pack began a cacophony that moved closer and closer to me. At first, I was arrested by what I thought was a beautiful energy emanating from their interaction. But, as they got closer, seemingly within 10 or 15 yards, I found myself pressing my pipe to my heart in fear. The closer they came, the more aggressive their yelping became. Suddenly, there was total silence. For a while, I could not even hear the breeze through the leaves. The short pause seemed like an eternity. I held my breath to hear. Then, I heard movement of maybe one coyote in the bushes and grass at a very close proximity. Then, suddenly I heard the pack run away toward the southwest. I was drenched in sweat. I reflected that I never had anything to fear from the coyotes. Whoever heard of scrawny coyotes hurting anyone? But they could be aggressive in packs. My mind wanted to make meaning of the experience. I was a little afraid and I had become alert and focused for 10–30 min while the coyotes yelped. I remembered that Edger Allen Poe said somewhere that the times we are terrified are the most real moments of our lives. I tried to relax into and appreciate the "realness" of those moments without bracing myself.

Later, sometime in the early morning hours, I heard something moving in starts and stops in the rustling leaves, again moving toward me. I breathed as quietly as I could, attempting to discern any noise that might help me identify what it was. I considered that it might be some person, but then thought why would a person walk through these briars and thickets to get to the top of this hill. Then, I heard a bleat like a young deer. But, I considered it a deer only for a moment because the image of *Uktena*, the mythic Cherokee snake of the mountains emerged in my mind. The monster snake was known to make herky–jerky movements in the grass and make a sound like a deer in order to lure hunters into its lair. I chastised myself for allowing my imagination to run away with me. Maybe, it was a spirit. I spoke my name and asked who it was. No answer. After a few moments I heard it move away from me. I thanked it for its company.

The darkness seemed to last for hours and hours. I considered how my sense of time was considerably "off." When I lay back, I enjoyed the view of the stars, as they moved across the sky. I found the Milky Way and the Big and Little Dippers. But, I realized that I would become drowsy unless I sat up Indian cross-legged. The early morning was quiet. I became enveloped by the darkness and experienced a mindful sense of simply being. I did not get sleepy.

Eventually, I began to see the natural environment around me. I first felt disappointed because I was expecting to see the sun climb up over the eastern horizon. Instead, gray clouds lined the horizon. It was an hour or two before I saw the sun, which was a bright yellow light instead of an orange globe. Nonetheless, I began singing a Cherokee sunrise song when I saw its first bright rays. During the first verse, I felt happy but during the second verse, I closed my eyes and was terrified with a series of images of Cherokee families being jerked from porches by cavalry soldiers. I saw Cherokees dressed in "White people's" clothes of the 1830s sick and dying in wagons, some being buried in shallow graves along trails. I was crying as I finished the song. I sang a Choctaw Walk song as I turned counterclockwise to the south. I saw similar horrific nineteenth century scenes of Choctaws on their Trail of Tears. I turned to the West and saw nineteenth century soldiers burning peach trees and herding Navajos away from their homes. I recited a Navajo "Walk in Beauty" chant. As I turned to the North, I considered that I had no more tears to offer. I was dehydrated and exhausted. But, I heard an inner voice that told me to hold the pipe toward the north and to sing a Lakota *chanupa* (pipe) song. I did not want to close my eyes. When I did, I heard gunshots and I felt cold. I saw Indians lying dead on a cold winter day. A man's hair was long. There was a woman shot through the chest. They looked cold, left there on the frozen ground. I wanted to cover them. I heard my voice singing the pipe song and it was profoundly mournful. I wanted to stop singing but a voice told me that it was healing for them and for myself to complete it. I was utterly exhausted as I collapsed on the earth. There was a hawk high in the sky above me, the first of many I would see throughout the vision quest.

Again, time stopped. The sun seemed to stay in the same place. The hotter and thirstier I became, the more frustrated I became with *Hashtali* (Choctaw word for sun). There I sat, my head ducked down, protecting my eyes from the bright light. There was absolutely no shade. I guessed it was near 100°. I was pretty tanned, having made a point to wear the same gym shorts in the sun the last couple of weeks, hoping to protect myself from sun burn, but I felt like my skin was melting away. As the sun hovered interminably, my thirst grew in intensity. At one point, I had the epiphany that the sun, *Hashtali*, was much more than a ball of fiery energy. Choctaw elders had told me the truth of this awareness many times during sweat lodge ceremonies but I never really considered what they were taking about. They called the sun the Governor sometimes. I suddenly experienced the sun as a living, feeling, and conscious entity. Choctaws had been called sun worshippers. And, I had always corrected those who quoted this idea from books like it was a fact. But now, I did not think it was so blasphemous. An inner voice told me that people who thought they worshiped the true God typically worshiped a lower demigod who was many levels below God. I was moving in and out of experiencing a relationship with the sun and then feeling that I was the sun. Its light as well as its heat seemed to penetrate me. Its light illuminated everything, not only allowing me to see other things in nature but also filling my awareness with an extraordinary purity and intense ecstasy. For as long as 30 min or more, my breathing was energized by euphoria, until I became exhausted.

Now I was thirsty, really thirsty. I imagined drinking an entire gallon jug of water. I typically drink a lot of juices and sodas but now I wanted water. I laid down in a fetal position hoping that the searing hot 100-degree rays of sun would have less skin to burn. But, the heat on my back and side coupled with thirst was making me crazy. I emptied my bucket and sat on it. I closed my eyes and concentrated on each breath I took. My monkey mind kept intruding and I thought of how difficult it must be for people with cancer to meditate when they are in such pain. Gradually, I began to turn off my obsessive mind, returning to a focus on my breath. I relaxed for a long time. But, eventually I rolled off the bucket, and I remember trying to lick my totally parched lips. Again, I wanted to be in charge of the situation. I wanted water and I wanted it now. Yet, something told me that I had to learn to surrender to the process and believe that everything would be ok. Though the experience was excruciating, I had the thought that I was going through a process of healing.

I heard drums of war in my head. The Choctaws only used drums in times of war. It was a loud, fast drumbeat, maybe a hundred times a minute. I started singing, "Hey, hey, hey, sac - ri - fice. Hey, hey, hey. Sac - ri - fice." Over and over I sang the song. I looked up to the sky and saw a hawk circling. Then, I heard a noise, a ruffling in the dirt coming up the hill. I closed my eyes. I knew it was Wiley Coyote bringing me the traditional small glass of medicine tea. I never opened my eyes until he was gone. I picked up the glass and drank it in the smallest sips, trying to make it last. It was so little, but I appreciated it. I had a deep appreciation for Wiley remembering me and believing in me. I appreciated the Cherokee quester for reminding me to see everything, even every sip of tea as sacred.

Just before it was growing dark, I watched at least a hundred bats slam into the limbs of a couple of oak trees about 20 yards to my south. They appeared to be coming out of a cave in a ravine 75 yards southeast of my prayer circle. They hung upside down. When they hit the tree limbs, they swung from an upside down position, back and forth. I was fascinated but a little afraid. Unlike my first vision, during which I knew what I was seeing was in my mind's eye, now I was not for sure if I was actually in a spiritual dimension. I was seeing the "bats" with my physical eyes. But, everything around me had an "air of unreality" about it. Wiley Coyote had specifically picked this place out for me for its sanctity, or its capacity to attune itself to me. I thought, "Are there supernatural entities who reside here." My tribal people contend that there are spiritual manifestations connected with certain areas of the living earth. I have heard elders speak of spirits emerging from underground. The bats appeared to come from a cave. I considered how the bat was a perfect symbol of a creature that bridged the physical and spiritual dimensions. Could they have emerged from a cave to reveal spiritual knowledge to me?

Sleep became too hard to resist. I dozed off. A vivid Technicolor dream vision came to me. I was playing left field, 250 feet from the batter. One hundred and fifty feet behind me there was a tight barbed wire fence held up by rustic fence posts. The teenagers and young adults playing on both teams of this softball game went to a Southern Baptist Church I once attended. Eagle Beak was at bat. He hit the pitch high in the air my way. I ran all the way back to the barbed wire fence but it soared far beyond, finally hitting in a level pasture land covered with short buffalo grass. I quickly spread the top two prickly wires and climbed through the fence barely avoiding cuts. I ran behind the bouncing softball that traveled only slightly faster than my full gallop. I raced across a forty-acre grassland pasture toward an oilfield road where there was situated an old farmstead house. Its paint had vanished long ago and its porch and stairway were rickety. The ball hopped across the road, up each of the three stairs and then through the open front door. I halted before the house, considering the risks of entering this old "abandoned" house. I summoned up my courage and entered. There was a man in front of a bar and another behind it. They both wore old black suits and hats. The man behind the bar had the softball in his right hand. I stood speechless on bare floor planks in the middle of the room. No one spoke for several seconds. The man behind the bar assumed the voice of Groucho Marx and said with utter finality, "Rockey, it is not that you shouldn't be afraid; it's that there is nothing to be afraid of."

Again, the morning sky was gray for the first couple of hours after sunrise. The bats were still in the trees. When *Hashtali* finally did break through with intense light and heat, the natural environment around me was illuminated unlike anything I had ever seen. In a tree east of me, there was a gigantic spider web, contained within a dead branch that had curved itself into an almost perfect circle. *Hashtali* shone through it. I was utterly enchanted by its beauty. I observed every detail for an unknown amount of time. Later, I found myself digging my fingers into the sandy brown earth. It felt cool between my fingers. I imagined how life had been emerging from the miraculous dirt. It was my mother, and she was always there beneath me, holding me, much like my human mother had always held me.

About noon, my supporters came back to retrieve me to the lodge. As before, I was wrapped up from the knees to the head in a Pendleton blanket. I pointed to the one hundred bats in the oak trees, wanting everyone to see such a spectacular sight. Nothing was said all the way back to the lodge until everyone was seated around the sacred stones. I told those who supported me of much of what I had seen. We sweat two rounds. We three questers then sat in folding chairs outside the lodge and drank bottled water. Then, we burned our prayer ties, letting the prayers ascend. At lunch, I could only eat watermelon. I did not feel like talking to anyone. In fact, I talked little for the entire day, even at my own house. I just sat in a sofa. I did not want to hear a television or radio. I remember at one point my son kept pressuring me for something, and I raised my voice at him. I immediately felt ashamed and thought of how contradictory my angry behavior was, having just sat in a spiritual space for so long. My wife had everyone simply give me space. They also fixed meals for me and talked quietly for the rest of the day. After 4 days, I found myself fully in the world again, though with a new perspective. I felt humbled, and I wanted to live in a more mindful way, careful to treat every person and animal I encountered as sacred.

Over the next few years, both my wife and son would go on vision quests. We supported each other, participating in all the sweats leading up to them. The ongoing preparation and the event itself joined us in a common cause. It kept us in a special state of united mindfulness in regard to our attitudes toward each other and our everyday actions. The upcoming vision quests, which we regarded as spiritually significant, helped us to sustain a balance and restraint in our individual lives and a kindness toward others. We also felt blessed that we could participate in such spiritual rituals, knowing that outside our community, such spiritual schooling is rare.

Community Embrace of Solitary Search

Much has been written about the communal character of traditional Native American life. Even the apparent solitude in the above narrative is embedded in fellowship. The vision quest actually demonstrates a balance between solitude and fellowship. To have sought solitude without embracing my connections would have been vain, pretentious, and self-delusional. On the other hand, to have never sought solitude would leave me with nothing unique to offer my community. My family members who shared tribal values pulled together to support me and I, having completed my vision quest, could contribute to the revitalization of our relationships.

My son and wife had to bear with my separation from them, and the requirement of the vision quest may at times have taken them away from things they wanted to do. They committed themselves to the involvement of my seemingly solitary reality with great patience and ultimately with joy. They not only prepared me for the quest itself, but supported me in my reentry in everydayness by giving me time and space to integrate my experience and eventually to facilitate my talking through many of the mysterious happenings.

Community members also supported me with advice and with careful, empathetic listening. When I was uncertain or discouraged, they were attentive. When I felt especially vulnerable, Wiley Coyote soothed me with comforting words. I learned to trust him profoundly. Those who stayed at the encampment praying for me helped me to cope with an experience that was too big for me alone. Further, their choosing to witness my precarious journey connected me more profoundly to them because it aroused deep appreciation. I realized that my life has and never will be solely dependent on my own resources.

Emotions and Mental Health

Emotions can become maladaptive when overlearned in response to crisis or reinforced in multiple, often paradoxical, ways. I was surprised that fear became a predominant theme through my vision quest. For most of my life, I have been a strong, muscular man, unafraid of any physical attack. Nor have I anticipated frightful things that might occur in my life. I was not really scared while I was on my vision quest, but I think I felt fear on a primary, often unconscious level. One of my gifts is in conceptualization and in analysis, involving making comparisons and judgments. Putting so much effort in controlling and predicting, I might have kept fear of the unpredictable and irrational at arm's length. As a consequence, this fear, unacknowledged, may have contributed to illusory perceptions that those I am judging and objectifying are separate from me, making it difficult for me to truly love them. In addition to damaging my relationships, my fear also interfered with my peace of mind, as I tried to control things and people in order to keep them moving in predictable patterns. During the vision quest, I had no choice but to respond spontaneously to the unpredictable.

I wonder now about the role that pain played in the release of my inner secrets. I experienced physical privation, loneliness, and grief. Many mystics (Underhill, 1955) argue that we tend not to change characterologically except in response to pain. C.S. Lewis (1962) wrote, "Suffering is not good in itself… but the human spirit will not even begin to try to surrender self-will as long as all is seen as well with it." The disorientation I felt because of the esoteric as well as the painful nature of the ritual put me in a place where I was open to imagery and symbolism that was psychologically transformative. As long as my selfish self was in control, I experienced fear of individual destruction, but when I opened myself up to my more universal, interconnected self, I was released from that fear. During the vision quest, symbols emerged without my conscious manipulation and released deep inner fears and some of the physical pain. The images and symbols of my visions and dreams that lay behind my intangible emotions gave my mind something concrete to better understand myself and my relationship to family members and everything that lives.

Imagining Respectful Caring for Nonmainstream Spiritual Experience

As I reflect on my experience, I can imagine how culturally sensitive practitioners could have helped my family and me in the aftermath. The *DSM-V* (American Psychiatric Association, 2013) lists "Brief reactive psychosis" in the Culture-Bound Syndromes section as potential reactions to spiritual practices. While this represents an advance in our helping professions accepting transpersonal experiences as potentially transformative, it does not sufficiently differentiate pathological from transpersonal experiences. Caroline Brett (2010) argued that the two types of experiences are similar but a therapist must take into account the context and outcome. Further, a person may be experiencing both pathological and transpersonal experiences. The extent to which therapists can successfully discern as well as appreciate the experience is vital. Success in therapy depends on the therapist's capacity to validate the client in her/his experience. This is why, family therapy is crucial at least intermittently with persons who bring in this type of experiences to sessions. Family members can often help validate the relevance of the experiences to the cultures they live in.

A therapist who works with persons experiencing spiritual crisis should know, at bare minimum, the levels of spiritual development proposed by Underhill (1955), Fowler (1981), and Wilber (2007). I would have felt uncomfortable with a therapist who simply assumed that they were able to ask intelligent questions and offer understanding support, if they were unfamiliar with writers who appreciated states and stages of awareness. Underhill described state–stage challenges and achievements along a spiritual path from a mystical Christian perspective. Fowler objectively examined large numbers of peoples' spiritual journeys and demarcated them into distinctive stages of development, from a Liberal Christian perspective. Wilber attempts to match up spiritual development with cognitive, moral, identity, and emotional developmental models. His integral model takes into account Eastern mystical spiritual development models as well. Though none of the models address Native American spiritual journeys, there are resonances, and if a therapist had knowledge of these models, they would have been more likely to articulate about the challenges I faced, to ask more relevant questions, and able to help me with a treatment plan.

While I was eventually able to get reconnected to everyday activities, talking to a competent family therapist could have been beneficial. For at least 4 days after my vision quest, I talked little to anyone, was tearful, and was zoned out or distracted much of the time. I needed to be reminded that the "spiraling" would gradually level out. I recalled that Wiley Coyote had told me to expect this, but that if I remained "zoned out" beyond 4 days, we would have to have another sweat to help me come back from the spirit world. But alas, my wife and son helped me to come back to this world. On the fifth day, they had me walking the dog twice a day, making salads, barbequing, and digging the weeds out of our vegetable garden. While each of these activities was helpful in itself, it was my family members' presence and conversations as they joined me in activities that helped to ground me. Therapists might recommend these types of joint activities to clients who may have had similar spiritual experiences.

While I wanted to be grounded, this did not mean I wanted to forget the lessons I had learned during the vision quest. As I look back at that time, I could have benefited from family therapy. I would have wanted to be able to talk about readjustments we might have to make and how everyone felt about it. I had new priorities and attitudes about my job and my spiritual perspectives. I wanted to involve myself in greater service for people of color. I also wanted to be more available and supportive of my family. I think many families could benefit from working with a therapist to help them work through these challenges of spiritual transition.

A therapist might also work with clients who wish to investigate the meaning of the symbolic language of their clients' spiritual experiences. If I had gone to a therapist to discuss the meaning of my experience, I would have wanted a therapist who would allow me, for the most part, to construct my own meanings. Still, it would have been helpful if the therapist were capable of making parallel associations to Native American beliefs and stories, world literature, and religious writings. Again, allowing for my own interpretations, I would have also appreciated their insights about recurrent themes. I would not have appreciated a therapist who restricted and reduced the symbols to sexual and parental relational interpretations. For instance, a therapist may have helped me to connect the spider web I saw in the tree limb with my mother and I would have been fine with that, knowing that the spider recurs in association with mothers throughout the world literature, but should be careful not to impose meanings counter to my tribal worldview.

We might consider some of the questions that might have been helpful in understanding the dream I had during the morning hours of the last night of the vision quest. What do you associate with the pastoral setting of the softball game? What about the old house the ball bounced into? Why do you think a comedian told you that there was nothing to be afraid of? How do you think this dream is related to the bird that fell into your circle? Do you knock yourself out for anything? What recurring themes do you see in the dreams and visions?

Rereading my description, I see that several themes appear to run through it. I wonder, were you my therapist, if you might be considering similar ones to discuss in sessions: Family emotional dynamics, such as time and place for hard and soft feelings, balance of individuality and participation in tribal contexts, relationship to mother and father, geographic attunement, the supernatural, cross-cultural textuality, kinds of fear, death, visionary experience, mental and emotional flexibility, time and no-time, earth mother, reality–nonreality, control, community, atonement, being and becoming, thankfulness, good in apparent evil, pauses, and awareness in everything that lives.

To be a responsible therapist requires knowing enough about the client and their culture to support them intelligently along their cultural/spiritual path. While the client may teach a therapist some things about his/her culture, therapy must be more than a learning experience for the therapist. In fact, a tribal client may be hesitant to share tribal ways with someone not in their tribe and certainly with someone who knows nothing about their life world. Consultation with persons who have deeper knowledge of tribal/spiritual issues, e.g., tribal elders might be needed.

Conclusion

As you read my words, know that you and I stand on land where Native Americans once roamed freely. The time came when our cultural/tribal capitals were wrested away and we were often moved forcibly to areas far from our areas of ethnogenesis. The vision quest was miraculously preserved by many tribes, though I am especially appreciative of the generosity of the Lakota, who provided me with a space and a guiding ritual to attain a spiritual awakening. If my story has touched your heart, please recognize my trepidation and trust in sharing with you from our traditions that have been demonized, trivialized, and caricatured by colonialists who tried but failed to destroy us. Please make a place at the table of spiritual paths for our spiritual traditions.

References

American Psychiatric Association. (2013). *Diagnostic and statistical manual of mental disorders: DSM-5* (5th ed.). Washington, DC: Author.

Brett, C. (2010). Transformative crisis. In I. Clarke (Ed.), *Psychosis and spirituality: Consolidating the new paradigm* (155–174). Hoboken, New Jersey: Wiley-Blackwell.

Fowler, J. W. (1981). *Stages of faith*. San Francisco: Harper Publishers.
Hill, P. C., & Pargament, K. I. (2003). Advances in the conceptualization and measurement of religion and spirituality: Implication for physical and mental health research. *American Psychologist, 58*(1), 64–74.
James, W. (1902/1982). *The varieties of religious experience*. New York: Penguin.
Jung, C. G. (1961/1983). *Memories, dreams, reflections*. London: Fontana Paperbacks.
Lame Deer, J., & Erdoes, R. (1972). *Lame Deer seeker of visions*. New York: Simon and Shuster.
Lewis, C. S. (1962). *The problem of pain*. New York: McMillian Publishers.
Otto, R. (1958). *The idea of the holy*. Oxford: Galaxy Books.
Underhill, E. (1955). *Mysticism*. New York: Meridian Books.
Wilber, K. (2007). *Integral spirituality*. Boston: Integral Books.

A Conversation in Sacred Space

David Trimble, Khawla Abu-Baker, Kiran Arora, Saliha Bava, Paulette Hines, Hugo Kamya, Jay King, Linda Longo-Lockspeiser, and Rockey Robbins

> If you cast yourself into the sea, without any guidance, this is full of danger, because man mistakes things that arise within himself for things arising from elsewhere. If, on the other hand, you travel on the sea in a ship, this is perilous, because there is the danger of attachment to the vehicle. In the one case, the end is not known, and there is no guidance. In the other case, the means becomes an end, and there is no arriving.
>
> —Niffari (Quoted in Shaw)

> Angels can fly because they can take themselves lightly
>
> —Chesterton

We invite you to imagine that you are sitting in a circle with others, some of whom you may know, some of whom you are meeting for the first time. As the "talking stick" passes from person to person, each speaker responds to this charge: "Share

D. Trimble (✉)
Center for Multicultural Training in Psychology, Division of Psychiatry, Boston University School of Medicine, Boston, MA, USA

Boston Institute for Culturally Affirming Practices, Boston, MA, USA
e-mail: d.trimble@earthlink.net

K. Abu-Baker
Alqasemi College of Education, Baqa, Israel

Western Galilee College, USA

K. Arora
Long Island University, Brooklyn, NY, USA
e-mail: kiran.arora@liu.edu

S. Bava
Marriage and Family Therapy Program, Mercy College, Dobbs Ferry, NY, USA

Houston Galveston Institute, Houston, TX, USA

Taos Institute, Chagrin Falls, OH, USA

D. Trimble (ed.), *Engaging with Spirituality in Family Therapy*, AFTA SpringerBriefs in Family Therapy, https://doi.org/10.1007/978-3-319-77410-7_9

with us something about yourself that will help us to get to know you. Tell us how you understand your own unique personal experience of spirituality, including, if relevant, with what religious community you may identify. Tell us a story of your work; a story of how your work is shaped by your life and by your spiritual practice." Because the speakers are identified in some way or another with family therapy, the stories you hear may span generations of the speakers' lives. As you prepare for your turn, notice how the words that you will speak are shaped and transformed by your own experiences of ancestors, spirituality, and complex intersectional identities, and, also, by the stories that you are witnessing as others speak.

Welcome to the conversation among the authors. All of us are committed to cultivating an ethical dialogical meeting place, in which we can resonate with our diverse particular experiences without seeking consensus, or feeling compulsion to agree with particular beliefs. Because one aim of our project is to imagine a global discourse grounded in spirituality, our conversation must remain open to the diversity of forms of human spiritual and religious expression.

Some of us understand imagination to be an entryway to realms beyond the world of everyday experience and believe that gaining access to nonmaterial worlds is a form of spiritual practice. We invite you to imagine, without having to "believe," that our conversation, which in everyday linear time has been going on among us for three years, sometimes face to face, sometimes by video, mostly by e-mail, is taking place in the present, and in a place, that are beyond the limitations of space and time.

P. Hines
Department of Psychiatry, Rutgers Robert Wood Johnson Medical School, Rutgers University Behavioral Health Care (Emerita), Piscataway, NJ, USA

H. Kamya
School of Social Work, Simmons College, Boston, MA, USA

Boston Institute for Culturally Affirming Practices, Boston, MA, USA
e-mail: hugo.kamya@simmons.edu

J. King
Palo Alto University, Palo Alto, CA, USA

Boston Institute for Culturally Affirming Practices, Boston, MA, USA
e-mail: jayking@paloaltou.edu

L. Longo-Lockspeiser
Private Psychotherapy Practice, Valley Stream, NY, USA

R. Robbins
Department of Educational Psychology (Counseling), University of Oklahoma, Norman, OK, USA
e-mail: rockey@ou.edu

The Conversation Begins

Now, each of us has spoken, passing the talking stick to the next author after our chapter in this book has finished. We have listened respectfully to your, the reader's, own story. As we set the talking stick aside for a cross-conversation, we pause to focus on our breathing. We contemplate the challenge and the obligation we face. We are taking on the paradoxes embodied in criticizing an individualistic global culture, and making the claim for a global human culture that affirms spirituality. We know the history of violent struggle for supremacy by many religions, including, for some of us, our own. In our effort to assert the fundamental importance of spirituality for life on the planet, we recognize the peril of lapsing into a universalizing monologue. How do we articulate an understanding that truly embodies dialogue? Russian thinker Mikhail Bakhtin (Bakhtin, 1981), who, in the Soviet era, could not afford to be explicit about his religious faith, asserted that meanings emerge in the space between the speaker and the listener. Dialogue is generative and continuous. It can be interrupted, but never ends as long as there is a relationship between the speaker and the listener. We reflect on the subtle wisdom in Niffari's words, quoted at the beginning of this chapter, knowing that we need to have some form in which to hold our spiritual experiences but recognizing the peril of clinging to our forms. As we stay open to each other's words, our experiences of spirituality are continuously renewed. We bear in mind Chesterton's aphorism (also at the beginning of this chapter), and try not to take ourselves too seriously in our mutual search for understanding of phenomena that are ultimately beyond the reach of our words.

Spirituality and Language

As we engage with the manifold forms of human spiritual tradition, we are grateful for our comfort with paradox, one vital root of the branching tree of family therapy. Many of us have struggled with writing about experiences that are intrinsically beyond the limits of language. Words make distinctions, and distinctions can feel contrary to experiences of a Unity beyond all limitations. How is it possible to share our experiences with each other, without using the vehicle of language? How to hold to that vehicle lightly enough to "arrive" at an "end" that is deeply personal and beyond description? Somehow, we find rich language to engage with each other about experiences intrinsically beyond the limitations of language.

Our conversation draws on Rivett and Street's (2001) distinction between "instrumental" and "metaphysical" interventions, words that we have found useful in our work. As useful as the distinction may be when making clinical decisions, we are finding how lightly we actually hold that distinction in our work. In their chapters, Paulette describes invoking Christian aphorisms to help her patients work toward their goals of growth and personal healing; Hugo describes his healing work with refugees, co-constructing with them metaphors grounded in African spiritual beliefs and practices; Khawla works indirectly with Sheikhs to help Nuha free herself from possession; David translates esoteric ideas from Judaism into Christian theological terms to help Gracia liberate herself from negative influences; Kiran studies the texts of Guru Nanak with Bani, collaborating with her to interpret the beliefs of Sikhism in Bani's current complex social and cultural context. One could characterize all these interventions as instrumental, as they draw on patients' existing beliefs and practices, helping patients to employ them to make therapeutic progress. Yet they are, for us, also inescapably metaphysical, as they activate spiritual beliefs and practices that we share with our clients. We often live in the same spiritual meaning systems as our clients, and are affected by the words that we utter. Both Khawla and David, for example, took care to protect ourselves from the nonmaterial entities tormenting our patients.

We play with Rivett and Street's ambiguous phrase, "the same, and different, and the same," which we find suits our efforts to acknowledge our common experiences of spirituality, embodied in the very different particulars of our faiths and practices. Useful but difficult to grasp, the phrase offers us a perspective as we seek words for experiences beyond words. We respect that each religious tradition operates within its own frame of reference, and that its richest meanings may emerge from within those frames of reference. We write to Mark Rivett and Eddy Street, and Eddy responds, [1] "For me this [the same and different and the same] is like a Zen koan…. We are here alluding to a way of orienting to phenomena given the non-dual nature of the universe…. Spirituality and psychotherapeutic practice have differences but are contained within the same universal process of (shall be say,) 'becoming'…" We express our gratitude to Jay, whose nondualistic practice of the Tao helps us to grasp, and to let go of, the meanings in "the same and different and the same." Hugo comments, "My first reaction to this is: the importance of seeking the familiar in the strange and the strange in the familiar. Or simplicity in complexity as we seek complexity in simplicity. In the end complexity and simplicity continually unfold complexity and simplicity. Maybe when we think we have arrived at something we are called to seek to find a beginning. All of this evokes for me what Bakhtin speaks of as 'the unfinalizability' of voices."

Paulette invites us to listen to an audio link,[2] a reading from the words of Neale Donald Walsch (Walsch, 2005), a contemporary teacher who shares his experiences of Divine revelation. We listen to and reflect on these words, offered in the voice of God:

> When we try to speak to each other… we are immediately constricted by the unbelievable limitation of words…. I do not communicate by words alone…. My most common form of communication is through feeling...… I also communicate with thought…. Thoughts and feelings are more effective than mere words as tools of communication. … Words are really the least effective communicator…. They are not truth. They are not the real thing….Now the supreme irony here is that you all place so much importance on the word of God, and so little on the experience. In fact, you place so little value on what you experience that when your experience of God differs from what you have heard of God, you automatically discard the experience and own the words, when it should be just the other way around…

---

[1] Street, personal communication, August 24, 2017.

[2] http://www.audible.com/t2/title?asin=B002VA3J6Y&source_code=GO1GBSH09091690EI&mkwid=szqA7GtPz_dc&pcrid=205747089334&pmt=e&pkw=conversations%20with%20god&cvosrc=ppc.google.conversations%20with%20god&cvo_campaign=250472289&cvo_crid=205747089334&Matchtype=e&gclid=EAIaIQobChMIrea7vMjL1QIVAgRpCh2EmA_mEAAYASAAEgIrX_D_BwE.

Our conversation gets animated as we reflect on Walsch's teaching. Paulette says, "I have wondered if my struggle to respond to so many of the questions posed during this writing project has been in part because I connect with the power of my spirituality more often through feelings and experiences that defy words." Linda responds, "I can absolutely relate to Paulette's observation. I have been grappling with the task of explaining the experience of Constellations without making it sound trite. Words limit the experience. So much of what happens is through ritual, and, as such is beyond words. The felt experience of the participants is often described simply as 'peace.'"

David's reaction is also strong, but he resists our coming to a consensus. He says, "I feel tension between agreeing/accepting on the one hand, and disagreeing/rejection on the other. I am thankful for Jay's presence, encouraging me to hold the tension without drawing conclusions, and appreciate the grace in words from his chapter, 'embrace an interactive and absorbing dialogue with other theologies.' Having participated as a representative in a Constellation exercise that Linda led, I know from experience a wordless knowing that guided me to bring into the room the presence of a physically absent person. Yet, I struggle with Walsch's conclusive statements that so strongly dismiss the spiritual importance of language, particularly as I hear the statements uttered in an authoritative White male voice. From a *Kabbalistic* perspective, constriction and limitation are positive, not negative processes. God becomes accessible to human awareness through a process of constriction that reduces the brilliance of Divine light, making it perceptible to the soul. Further, language is fundamental to Jewish theology and mythology, even as ultimate spiritual Truth is acknowledged to be beyond all description in language. In esoteric Jewish thought, the Torah existed in God's mind before Creation, and is Creation's design. It is hard for me as a Jew to reject language, when the world itself is seen as an embodiment of the sacred letters of the Hebrew alphabet! Judaism is not the only faith with reverence for language. Consider the initial words of the Christian Gospel of Saint John (John 1: 1-4, RSV), which resonate with Jewish myths of the role of language ("the Word") in creation: 'In the beginning was the Word, and the Word was with God, and the Word was God. He was in the beginning with God; all things were made through him, and without him was not anything made that was made.'"

Khawla reminds us of her account of her dying sister sharing with the family what she had been told by dead relatives who promised to accompany her to the next life. Members of the family gathered around Khawla's sister did not speak of what she was telling them, "since our socialization does not teach us terminology that may contain this type of spiritual experience in life. Many unique human experiences, in all faiths, are ignored and disrespected because we do not create words for them."

The same and different and the same. Although we have not reached consensus about words (indeed, have sought to avoid the monologic risk of mutual agreement), we all acknowledge nameless yet achingly familiar sensations evoked so often for each of us in our community of souls assembled around the writing of this book. When our collective journey began, several of us chose to wait to read others' words until we had found the words to produce the early drafts of our chapters. When we began to dance together in language, securely rooted in the particulars of our own spiritual faiths and practices, we discovered new wellsprings of spirituality for ourselves. We delight in the flowing dynamic between turning inward to find words faithful to ourselves and to our spiritual communities, and turning outward to share those words with each other. Inward and outward, neither one nor the other yet both, we find experiential meaning for the words, "the same, and different, and the same." Our conversation moves fluidly between agreements and disagreements, respectful of our differences even as many of us become more firmly grounded in our religious beliefs and practices. Ancient words take on new meanings, and new words evoke profound experiences that resonate with the spirits of primordial ancestors.

Some of our traditions have secret words, or words whose utterance is forbidden. In Judaism, the most sacred name of God can never be uttered, and written only on parchment scrolls used in ritual worship. Observant Jews use the term *Hashem* (Hebrew for "the Name") to refer to it, and prayer book translations use the euphemism THE LORD. The word is a simultaneous rendering of the verb, "to be," in past, present, and future tenses. Thus, this name of God can be roughly translated as "Is, Was, Will be." Rockey shares a Choctaw word for a timeless time and spaceless space that is the source of all being, which for David resonates with *Ein Sof* in Jewish *Kabbalah*. Rockey is gracious and compassionate with David when he asks out of his ignorance how to spell the name, which Rockey rendered as "no time, no space" in an article he wrote about his medicine man's practice (Robbins, Hong, & Jennings, 2011). Rockey teaches us that the name is never written; it is a sacred word, which will not appear in any Choctaw dictionary. In fact, because it does not exist in ordinary reality, its pronunciation may change each time that it is spoken. We acknowledge that some sacred knowledge must be kept secret, as it loses its spiritual power if it is shared outside the boundaries of the rituals in which it is embedded.

As we dive deeply into a conversation about the role of language in spirituality, it may not surprise you that we don't take too much time to try to distinguish between the words, "religion" and "spirituality." The question as to which term applies to which human acts, beliefs, or feelings has a different meaning, and different answers, in different cultural contexts. Are traditional indigenous beliefs, for example, Native American or African, "religions," or are they ways of knowing and being in the world, not necessarily distinguishable as "spiritual" or "religious," from within their own frames of reference?

We take a moment to play with words, trying to come up with as many words as we can that may evoke experiences associated with religion and/or spirituality, as follows: abandonment, acceptance, Allah, awe, blessing, Buddha, burden, clean, commitment, community, companion, compassion, corruption, courage, curse, Divine, darkness, dread, emptiness, energy, fear, fullness, generosity, God, grace, gratitude, growth, guide, guilt, Guru, healing, heart, holy ground, hope, humility, impure, Jesus, intimacy, journey, knowing, light, love, mindfulness, Mohammed, obedience, obligation, openness, narrative, pain, perception, power, profane, pure, quest, redemption, release, remorse, renunciation, respect, responsibility, reverence, rituals, sacred, sacred space, seeking, sensing, shame, sin, stillness, struggle, suffering, Tao, touch, truth, transcendence, transformation, unclean, virtue, vision, voice, yearning… What experiences do these words evoke for you, and what words come to you that you might want to add to the list?

Finding, Creating, Entering Sacred Space and Time

Saliha speaks. Her words move us, literally moving our conversation into a new topical domain, and metaphorically moving us into deep states of inner contemplation: "Even as I hope that my words move you, I yearn to learn the meaning of those words in your responses, and know that the creative, generative process (perhaps the portal to the spirit world?) requires that we never settle or rest on the words alone." Her words, "spirit world," open our conversation to considerations of sacred space and time, domains ultimately beyond the reach of language.

The Spiritans

For several years now, Hugo, Jay, David, and Pat Romney have met to consult about practicing therapy from a spiritual perspective. We dubbed our group the "Spiritans." Often, in the course of our conversations, we encounter experiences of awe and wonder, which we name moments of "transcendence." We have adopted Hugo's use of the term, "sacred space," (Kamya, 1999) to characterize our shared experience of entering domains beyond everyday experience. Physically separated, as we live long distances away from each other, the Spiritans assemble in sacred space using communication technology.

Paulette's words resonate with our description of Spiritans meetings, as she shares her experience of church services, when "Spirit enters the room." Linda says, "Rockey's experience, my friend's in Germany, and my own in countless Constellations as representative and facilitator confirm for me the reality of a spiritual dimension where time and space are irrelevant and where we are all connected."

The same, and different, and the same. We are engaging with you, Reader, in the "realm" of imagination, enabling you to participate in a conversation spanning several years as though in the same place at the same moment. Space and time are words, vessels that we must hold as lightly as we take ourselves. For many of us, spiritual reality incorporates spaces and times beyond the limitations of the material world. Somehow, we recognize it when our conversation takes us into sacred space. One of us offers the words, "We sojourners are resting in a beautiful, safe, open field to share our experiences of the journey."

Imagining Sacred Space in Global Culture

We treasure the moments when one, more, or all of us are moved spiritually. As one of us speaks from the heart about the particulars of their faith practice, the rest of us enjoy richer and deeper experiences of the particulars of our own spirituality. Hugo shares how his spiritual experience is enriched by our "internested conversations." How can we draw from our experiences together, and from what we know as family therapists, to support cultural evolution that builds universal access to sacred space? How do we understand engaging with our clients from a spiritual perspective?

Citing Saliha's and Kiran's lives as well as her own, Khawla reminds us that many in the world struggle against political and cultural limitations that bar their access to such experiences of sacred space. In the face of such stress, Khawla reminds us, "Some people then become reactive instead of active and end with using the politics of faith instead of focusing on their faith." Hegemonic religions disqualify outsiders, relating to them as "nonbelievers" who must either be converted or kept away. Hugo reminds us how his traditional African beliefs and practices are disparaged by monotheistic religions. Within religions, guardians of orthodoxy stifle coreligionists' efforts to cultivate their own particularities of spiritual practice.

Consider the geographical space of Israel and Palestine, holy to the three Abrahamic religions of Judaism, Christianity, and Islam, but often not the sacred space that we experience in our conversation. Polytheistic Romans, acting from secular imperial political considerations, exiled the Jews in the year 70 of the Common Era. The "Holy Land" came under the Muslim rule following military conquest. The Crusades marked another chapter in the bloody history of military conquest, as European Christians fought for and held territory for a few generations, until vanquished and expelled by Muslim armies. Centuries under the Muslim Ottoman Empire ended with European political occupation following the First World War, followed by the 1947 war that established Israel as a Jewish state, now in perpetual conflict with Muslim and Christian Palestinians, their common holy sites in Jerusalem at the center of an unstable truce punctuated by outbursts of bloody violence.

As you engage in this conversation, how can the case of this region inform your own generative thinking? Both as legacy and as painful present reality, the story of this region illustrates how faith can contribute to bloodshed and hatred. We are asking you to help imagine an alternative global culture that acknowledges universal human spirituality while respecting the destructive potential of hegemonic particularism. How can you respect your clients' particularism with compassion in your therapeutic conversations? How will you connect metaphysically with the spiritual reality of your clients' faith, without contesting or endorsing their assumptions of exclusive claim to the "Truth"?

A Role for Family Therapy

How can we, as family therapists, contribute to cultural change in a world where religion seems so often to obstruct, rather than facilitate, access to sacred space? Khawla asserts that, in parts of the world where economic forces shape "politics of faith," religion actually interferes with experiences of awe in response to natural or spiritual beauty. "War," says Khawla, "uses religion as a cover reason, hampers spirituality, divides mind from body, and religious communities one from the other." She challenges us further, "How can societies in the process of rapid social change draw on spirituality to help people adapt to change rather than suffer from alienation in the process? How can we challenge polarization of the spiritual and the secular that modernity forces on us? How do we resist rejecting parts of ourselves, including family, ancestors, education, culture, and self-esteem?"

Whether we called it "joining" (Minuchin, Nichols, & Lee, 2007) or "multipartiality" (Boszormenyi-Nagy, Grunebaum, & Ulrich, 1991), one of our first lessons as family therapists was to ally ourselves with all the members of a family, no matter how polarized among themselves; to see from multiple points of view. Could this stance somehow be integrated into an ethical global discourse of spirituality, marked by curiosity, mutual respect, and appreciation that the individuals engaged in dialogue across differences are deeply grounded in the particulars of their specific traditions?

Several of us align ourselves with the postmodern position, which stipulates that no one has an exclusive claim to the truth. Postmodern respect for the "local knowledge" of lived experience is consistent with appreciating the particulars of religious practices and beliefs, while resisting universal religious claims.

Dialogical practice (Andersen, 1991; Anderson, 1997; Seikkula & Olson, 2003), grounded in the implicit spirituality of Bakhtin's work (Bakhtin, 1981), affords both epistemological and ethical foundations for a global culture that acknowledges human spirituality. Collaborative and respectful dialogical practice seeks the meanings that emerge in the "space between" the speaker and the listener, a space that some of us experience as itself sacred space, particularly as feelings of love mark dialogical engagement in the space between (Seikkula & Trimble, 2005).

The counterpart of dialogue is monologue, attachment to a single perspective. Dialogue is not necessarily "good" in relation to monlogue as "bad"; each form has its utility in its context. Monologue is conclusive. Rational proof, systematic theology, scientific argument are examples of coherent monologue. Dialogue is generative, creating new meanings in the dialogic space between. Domination and competition between religions, and enforcement of orthodoxy within religions, are monologic practices, examples of "attachment to the vehicle" in the aphorism of Niffari's at the beginning of this chapter. Hugo and David share their compassionate exploration of the discourse of retaliation (Kamya & Trimble, 2002). We saw how the prospect of dialogue between adversaries, seen through the lens of trauma, appears dangerous. The discourse of retaliation is intrinsically a monologue, which eradicates the risk of engaging with the unpredictable subjectivity of the other.

David reflects on his experience with Artsbridge, a leadership-training program for young people living in conflict regions (Barzilay-Shechter, 2010; Nathan, Trimble, & Fuxman, 2015). Artsbridge combines training in the arts with a structured form of dialogue modeled on family therapist Tom Andersen's (1991) reflective approach. Supporting Palestinian and Israeli adolescents to develop language that bridges their embattled "space between" as they create intrinsically nonverbal works of art together affords them opportunities to discover new meanings. In using the vehicles of language and nonverbal experience, Artsbridge resonates with the conversation among us. Artsbridge training seldom results in one side persuading the other. Rather, it enables its students to listen respectfully, to be able to see through the eyes of the other. Years after the training, many Artsbridge graduates, now young adults, sustain relationships despite their differences, and remain committed to fostering dialogue. Given our interest in a discourse of spirituality that does not demand consensus, Artsbridge's use of dialogic theory from family therapy offers us hope. David's personal commitment to Artsbridge is grounded in a dream of reconciliation among embattled adherents of three religions, reconciliation with potential for enormous global influence.

Locating Sacred Space: The Same and Different and the Same

We reflect on the limitations of language as we contemplate the words, "sacred space." For some of us, the words may be metaphorical; others hold beliefs, grounded in the particularities of our religions, of worlds to come, of realms beyond the limitations of the material. As we concentrate on the meanings of the words, once again we encounter experiences of the same, and different, and the same. We talk of an internal experience of the sacred, recognizable but beyond words. Some of us feel ourselves "ascending" to spaces beyond ourselves, simultaneously accessing inner sacred space as we enter worlds beyond our individual embodiment. These very private experiences may emerge simultaneously for us during our conversation. The "space between" becomes a sacred space, which we acknowledge even as we accept that ultimately no words can capture these moments.

We wonder, is it possible to develop a common language for the diverse forms of engagement with spirituality in psychotherapy? Can we make any statement that does not imply a consensus, excluding alternative possibilities? We address these questions from a dialogical perspective, seeking to maintain a listening space for the "not yet spoken" (Seikkula & Arnkil, 2006). Among ourselves, we are familiar with "instrumental" approaches to helping our clients cultivate the healing potential of their religious and spiritual practices. We recognize that our own work incorporates something of the "metaphysical," since we all practice mindfully as self-reflective spiritual beings.

We are accustomed to inquiring about spirituality when we meet with new clients, and to helping them explore possibilities for healing and growth in their spiritual experience. It is not unusual for clients to tell us that they do not practice a religion but consider themselves to be spiritual. Inquiring about moments that clients consider to have been spiritual can uncover opportunities for instrumental and metaphysical healing.

We acknowledge that some clients firmly reject any exploration of the spiritual. Is there a way to engage with spirituality in such circumstances? Perhaps, without naming it as sacred space, we can nurture spiritual possibilities in the space between. Fully and authentically present with the other, we can also be mindful of our inner sacred space, thereby connecting with spiritual realms that are paradoxically beyond and within us. This affords us feelings of love that accompany the shift from monologic to dialogic forms of relational engagement.

Pain and Suffering

We recognize that our conversation must address "negative" experiences, even as we acknowledge Jay's Taoist perspective on the unity of all phenomena, good and evil, up and down, black and white, positive and negative. How can we respectfully address the phenomena of pain, suffering, oppression, guilt, and shame, and the problem of evil, within a spiritual framework?

Several of us speak of discomforts encountered in the process of writing our chapters. We share our feelings of uncertainty, comparing the quality of our writing with that of others, some associating this with a feeling of "not being good enough" that we acquired in our family's religions as children. We share past and (for some of us) present experiences of guilt over transgressing religious prohibitions or failing to respond to religious demands. Linda speaks about our struggles with doubt and fear, saying, "I think when I resist my morning practice, my prayer time, and my journal writing, what is operative is my fear that I will find nothing there—that I am on my own. That's the rational mind intruding and shaming the innocent child that knows from her heart that we are loved, cherished and cared for by a loving Presence that I call God."

We acknowledge that spirituality, particularly in the form of religion, can both comfort and afflict. Christianity and Islam have well-articulated ideologies of reward and punishment in the afterlife. A virtuous life assures eternal joy in the presence of God in Heaven; a sinful life is punished with the torments of Hell. Jewish prophetic literature explains the suffering of exile as a consequence of collective disobedience, and promises collective redemption for following the Law. All three Abrahamic religions temper their strict decrees with assurances of forgiveness and comfort from a compassionate God.

In our conversation, there is little talk about the problem of evil. Perhaps we implicitly recognize that there are culturally bound differences in our understandings of that term. We respect that some hold beliefs in a world embodying a cosmic struggle between good and evil, while others believe that all existence embodies a sacred, indissoluble unity.

We reflect on the problem, and the meaning, of suffering. We recognize the power of spirituality to comfort and soothe, to take people beyond the limitations of their own personal situations into broader perspectives that afford meaning, and the power of love in sacred space. We also acknowledge the suffering of people who may feel that they are not living up to the standards of their faith. Although none of us are practicing Buddhists, we are grateful for the teachings of the Buddha that recognize suffering as integral to the human condition, and that value detachment and compassion.

We ask the difficult question, "Is suffering itself integral to spiritual practice?" Christian theology assigns cosmic significance to Jesus's suffering, a deliberate act of redemption from sin for those who believe in him. Isaac Luria, the *Kabbalistic* spiritual master in sixteenth-century Sefirot, often prescribed fasting and other forms of self-deprivation for spiritual clarity (Fine, 2003). Mystics in many traditions practice asceticism. As we listened to Rockey's account of his experience of *Hanblechia,* we resonated with the painful sensations and emotions that framed his entrance into transpersonal experience.

Exploring this difficult theme of suffering makes us aware of the need for humility when we engage with clients about their spiritual experiences. We need to be openhearted, compassionate, and deeply respectful when we negotiate access to sacred space with people who are in pain about their religious lives, and whose beliefs may be very different from our own.

Responding to *An Interview with God*

(Editor's note: The following conversation embodies the practice of meeting dialogically in sacred space. Though the best way to engage with this section is to experience the video that we are discussing, what the authors wish for you to see is that, as different as our experiences are as we watch the video, each of us feels our own experience of spirituality become richer and deeper as we witness each other. The same, and different, and the same.)

Paulette shares another link to the work of Neale Donald Walsch.[3] In the video, breathtaking pictures of natural beauty are accompanied by moving, wordless music, and text that describes one of Walsch's encounters with his God, as follows:

> I dreamed I had an interview with God. "So would you like to interview me?" God asked. "If you have the time." I said.... "What surprises you most about humankind?" God answered..."That they get bored with childhood. They rush to grow up then long to be children again. That they lose their health to make money and then lose their money to restore their health. That by thinking anxiously about the future, they forget the present, such that they live in neither the present nor the future. That they live as if they will never die, and die as if they had never lived.".... I asked, "As a parent, what are some of life's lessons you want your children to learn?" God replied with a smile. "To learn that it is not good to compare themselves to others. To learn they cannot make anyone love them. What they can do is let themselves be loved. To learn that a rich person is not one who has the

[3] https://www.youtube.com/embed/moBvLFbFdJ4?rel=0&autoplay=1.

> most, but is one who needs the least. To learn that it only takes a few seconds to open profound wounds in persons we love, and it takes many years to heal them. To learn to forgive by practicing forgiveness. To learn that there are persons who love them dearly, but simply do not know how to express or show their feelings. To learn that two people can look at the same thing and see it differently. To learn that it is not always enough that they be forgiven by others. But that they must forgive themselves." ...."Is there anything else you would like your children to know?" "To learn that I am here. Always."

Walsch's words embody wisdom, and are not identified with a particular religion. Always the Editor in this conversation, David is concerned about the risk that Walsch's words could generate a monological consensus among us. He challenges each of us with the question, "Did watching the video activate your spirituality?" As we respond, we witness a polyphonic diversity of responses.

Kiran shares that she felt "calm and worry simultaneously. The images are serene and made me think of the vastness and unknowingness of God. I felt worry because although I agree with the answers God was giving and I believe them, I am not sure that I can carry the answers out better at the moment. I don't feel that watching the video activated my spirituality—but I am not sure of this. The worry kind of surprised me. Maybe given what is happening in the country and the world—I just am not sure how to slow down. That's all I have right now. Sitting with worry."

Khawla says, My first reaction was total appreciation and love to the pictured nature mixed with fear for the person who wants to interview God.... Nature shows the greatness of the creature, the greatness of God...we keep learning from God's messages and messengers to us. God teaches us that when we teach ourselves to appreciate the outside beauty in Nature and the inside beauty in our relation with ourselves and with others, then we will reach satisfaction of our experience in this life."

Saliha: "I was torn between the images and the words.... And in some ways, as I write, it strikes me that video could be a metaphor for the tension between the spiritual and the material. The images are so big and alive and in some way when one is in nature, I often find myself in what I would describe as in awe and in connection with something bigger. I can feel the incredible bigness that surrounds me and is unfathomable. I am in awe of how it all functions together, just like my body, in how it moves together. The mystery, beauty and the power of it all. So, the images in the video capture the spiritual while the words are the material life.... The words felt so human to me. How we make sense when we talk about 'money and health,' 'forgiveness,' 'time,' etc. It felt so cliché and yet if I allowed my mind to wander away from the critique, I could also hold the 'spirit' in the words, i.e. the meaning, the message.... And that right there is the reminder that in any one moment, there are so many voices and dichotomies. And yet being able to be, feel the tensions and see that all of it is in relationship to each other. The beauty is not only in the images only in that moment, but it is also in the tension, in the dichotomy that transforms itself into the dialectics—the tension in which each voice gets its definition by being in relationship to the other voices. That relationship is hard to fathom but often easier to experience as being in-tension (at least for me). I think that is the beauty of life, which is a fleeting moment of spirituality I believe.... So, in some strange contradictory way, maybe I am saying that this moment—the moment of making sense of the video—is the spiritual moment that got activated...."

Paulette: Initially, I was overwhelmed with the beauty of the natural 'wonders' depicted that represent the four corners of this earth, now and in the beginning of time; the extent to which the perfection portrayed is indisputably beyond human capacity to create; and the sense there is a relationship between all things. On second viewing, I became more aware of how challenging it is to attend to the words on the screen and the backdrop of the beautiful music and scenes simultaneously. I am left to wonder whether this tension mirrors our reality in some way. When I ponder the words, I tend to look inward, seeking to see whether there is any noticeable trend between what our human inclination leads us to do and what embracing our spirituality allows us to move toward. When I focus on the unspeakable beauty, I accept the imitations of my own understanding.

Linda: It gripped me immediately because of the beautiful video and music. Felt I could easily cry—with the fullness and magnificence and intricacy of nature's beauty. It transported me to my favorite space—Nature. Then, when the "conversation" began, my tears were more for how often I miss the mark—especially about wanting to grow up and then wanting to go back to childhood. If by spirituality, you are referring to that space that connects me to my Self, to God, to nature and to others, then yes, the video opened me up and got the energy flowing, making me feel more alive.

Hugo: I was filled with awe and wonder as I watched the video. There were many moments that each message brought me…. For me, I was transported in some of Henri Nouwen's work, *The Life of the Beloved* (1992), in which he explores spiritual living in a secular world. He discusses how one becomes the Beloved by exploring three moments: Taken, Blessed and Broken. To be Taken we have to remember that we can desire to become the Beloved only if we are already the Beloved. Therefore the first step in the spiritual life is to acknowledge with our whole being that we already have been taken. Indeed, as children of God, we are God's chosen ones. The word chosen kept speaking to me as I listened and watched the video. Indeed, that sense of specialness held me as I watched the video. I constantly feel thankful that God's graces continue through my life. This leads me to feel a sense of being blessed by all that God provides me. There are countless blessings in random acts of being. I cannot but stop thinking of my parents' blessing from long ago. I hold dear all the blessings that have come my way. These daily acts of affirmation and validation continue to give me the stubborn optimism that I so much cherish. But I also humbly appreciate that my life as a human being is broken which speaks to the continual learning and challenge that daily lies before me. My brokenness is an invitation to live humbly and to keep searching to learn beyond my small self. It is also an invitation to seek and find communion with others. This helps me appreciate who I am and who I am invited to become. It also offers me hope as I sit with the world's brokenness of the people I am called to serve especially those I speak about in my chapter.

David: I did experience sensations of transcendence as I read, looked, and listened to the video. Thanks to the personal transformations that I have experienced over the time that we have been writing, several of which I have written about in our email exchanges, I was far less ambivalent or frightened to allow myself the feelings of personal intimacy in an "interview" with God that the video evoked for me. By the time that I reached the end of the video, I was ready to take in the assurance from God, "I am always here." And yet, there was a part of me that wondered how this would land with someone who does not experience a God as a being in personal, intersubjective relationship with that someone.

Most of the ethical and mindfulness injunctions seemed and felt to me as universals; yet, again, I struggled with universals becoming monological impositions. I have saved the link, and plan to access it from time to time, to reconnect with my Spirit.

Rockey: I think that we are to learn to look through our eyes rather than with them. Maybe that is why, as the text says, "We get bored with childhood." We cease to use our childlike imaginations to interact with the beauty around us. I had the yearning to be in those environments as I watched them materialize and evaporate. While the paradoxes and wise words were beautiful I was distracted with the words. I wanted to absorb myself in the light that bathed the natural scenes. But then when it ended, I saw the morning sun dancing through the branches of my backyard tree. The light was making flickering designs on the back of a wicker chair in my room. Sometimes I need to be reminded to see the light. Thanks for the wonderful video that woke me up for a little while.

Jay: My initial reaction is profoundly spiritual and full of gratitude AND awareness of tsunamis, hurricanes and tornados, deserts and floods, the earthquakes and volcanoes that produce extraordinary and spectacular visions combined with catastrophic death and destruction (yin and yang).

Acknowledging Transformation

From a Bakhtinian perspective, conversation is "unfinalizable." Because each utterance derives its meaning from the response it evokes, conversations may be interrupted but they never finish. To join our conversation, you will need to read our words. Recognizing that we have to interrupt our conversation for our words to make their journey from the sacred space we are sharing into publication, we pause to reflect on whether and how our experiences of spirituality have changed over the three years we have been working together on this book.

Linda shares, "Being in our writing community this past year has been a blessing that confirms the innocent child in me…. My spirituality has not so much changed as it has deepened—I guess that is a change—as a result of our collaborative sharing. I have been at this place before where it is easy to see God in everything (immanence), but like all of life, this has come in cycles…God's Presence again reassuring me, reminding me not to take my life so seriously. It did not guarantee or spell out what would happen next, only that I was not alone and that truly it would all be ok…. Our process has inspired me—reigniting my spirit, removing internal obstacles to meditation, spiritual reading and journaling, and returning me to regular reception of the Eucharist mostly during the week…. I am reminded that 'everything belongs' and has a place in our incarnated life, that there is a mutuality in all that occurs…."

Rockey says, "I am so very grateful to be with all of you spiritual seekers. To sum it up, your journey has been a light to my own. My heart is filled with love and gratitude…. We need that strange element of love that hates that which is against love, righteous indignation. But we also need the awareness that God is in everyone. Just seeing that others are working on this just as I am is centering. Thanks for traveling on this boat with me for a while."

Kiran tells us, "I can feel myself growing and expanding over the course of working on the chapter with Saliha. While I have always identified as a Sikh, I have found myself much more curious about the intricacies of the words in our holy text, *Guru Granth Sahib.* I feel spiritually quieter as if I am on solid ground. I have more trust in things working out, in finding the answers that are meant for me. Reading others' chapters has reminded me of the threads that bind us together. I felt so many similarities between us as authors despite our different paths of spirituality. I feel hopeful and brave. I also find myself wishing we as people spoke more about faith and spirituality openly. I feel so connected to the authors through this dialogue, who else could I connect to? Where else can I create and nourish community that is inter-religion/spirituality and not just *intra*? I find myself wanting to translate some of the Sikh concepts to everyday modern life. This is easy to do but I haven't spoken much about spirituality, even with my Sikh clients. This is crazy!! Where and how did I learn not to do this? I am also wanting more contact with members of my faith community (not so many here in NYC) and it just occurred to me today that this yearning could be linked to the unraveling of my work in this book. I just looked up from my computer and saw a framed photo of the Harimandir Sahib (our most holy Gurudwara) on my wall. I bought and framed this photo in April—so many reminders of how I've added spiritual reminders in the past several months. I am grateful to be part of this journey. I want to continue expanding at the heart from what I am learning through this project."

David speaks. "As I read through the correspondence among the authors, I am struck again by the depth of personal, spiritual, emotional experience embodied in our words for each other…. I certainly am experiencing transformation in the process. A lifetime spiritual and emotional wound has marked my journey. God appeared to me in a dream when I was 9 years old, abandoned me, and left me with crushing responsibility. It was after an authors' videoconference that I experienced an assurance from God: Now having seen that I could carry on the work with which I had been charged, God would always be available in personal form as a Presence in my life. That has indeed happened. I think that, if God had called me in the way that S/He called my ancestors, I would have been a reasonably good Christian minister. The painful, paradoxical experience that I had in my personal relationship with God took me on another path, for which I am grateful…. I am sometimes moved to tears reading the words of my fellow authors, as I see the realization of a dream. We are engaged in deep conversation about our spirituality, activating Spirit in the space between our utterances, *without* being tempted to shape yet another religion. What I hope that we are shaping is a culture of respectful conversation between people deeply grounded in their own specific beliefs and practices. In so doing, we are contributing to the creation of a human culture that can some day replace the current soulless individualist global culture that is destroying humanity and the life of our planet."

Our Invitations to You

We hope that you are touched, as we are, by kaleidoscopic wonder at experiences grounded in the diversity of human religious, spiritual, and metaphysical traditions. May your experience of joining our conversation inspire you to reach out, explore within, and live your truth in relationship with the world and its peoples. As you engage with spirituality, we hope that you will find courage to address the problematic implications of religion and spirituality, for example, fundamentalism, particularism, and hegemonic aspirations. We hope to hear your voice as you contribute to a global discourse that respects universal human spirituality and celebrates the glorious particularism of human search for the Ultimate—not authoritative monologue, but generative dialogue.

We invite you to discover more of your own approach to making the therapeutic conversation a sacred space. How will you and members of the family in the room (and perhaps ancestors beyond the boundaries of the space and time of the room) engage in rich dialogue, each speaking from the particulars of their spiritual practice, as different as they may be from each other, so that all experience the familiar yet indescribable, the same and different and the same? As Saliha says, "I yearn to learn the meaning of those words in your responses, and know that the creative, generative process (perhaps the portal to the spirit world?) requires that we never settle or rest on the words alone."

References

Andersen, T. (1991). *The reflecting team: Dialogues and dialogues about the dialogues*. New York: Norton.

Anderson, H. (1997). *Conversation, language, and possibilities: A postmodern approach to therapy*. New York: Basic Books.

Bakhtin, M. M. (1981). In M. Holquist (Ed.), *The dialogic imagination: Four essays* (C. Emerson & M. Holquist, Trans.) Austin, TX: University of Austin Press.

Barzilay-Shechter, K. (2010). The Artsbridge group. *Journal of Applied Arts and Health, 1*(3), 333–339.

Boszormenyi-Nagy, I., Grunebaum, J., & Ulrich, D. (1991). Contextual therapy. In A. Gurman & D. Kniskern (Eds.), *Handbook of family therapy, volume II* (pp. 200–238).

Chesterton, G. K. (1959). *Orthodoxy*. New York: Doubleday Image Books (originally published in 1908 by Dodd, Mead, & Co.)

Fine, L. (2003). *Physician of the soul, healer of the cosmos: Isaac Luria and his Kabbalistic fellowship*. Stanford, CA: Stanford University Press.

Kamya, H. (1999). The landscape of spirituality in therapy. *The Bulletin of the Boston Institute for Psychotherapy, 3*(2), 12–17.
Kamya, H., & Trimble, D. (2002). Response to injury: Toward ethical construction of the other. *Journal of Systemic Therapies, 21*(3), 19–29.
Louwen, H. J. M. (1992). *Life of the beloved: Spiritual living in a secular world.* New York: Crossroad.
Minuchin, S., Nichols, M., & Lee, W. Y. (2007). *Assessing families and couples: From symptom to system.* Boston: Pearson/Allyn and Bacon.
Nathan, D., Trimble, D., & Fuxman, S. (2015). Building partnerships between Israeli and Palestinian youth: An integrative approach. *Israel Affairs, 21*(1), 148–164.
Rivett, M., & Street, E. (2001). Connections and themes of spirituality in family therapy. *Family Process, 40*, 459–467.
Robbins, R., Hong, J., & Jennings, A. M. (2011). In the pause and listening to the little people: A folk healer's journey. *The Counseling Psychologist, 40*, 93–132.
Seikkula, J., & Arnkil, T. E. (2006). *Dialogical meetings in social networks.* London: Karnac.
Seikkula, J., & Olson, M. E. (2003). The open dialogue approach to acute psychosis: Its poetics and micropolitics. *Family Process, 42*, 403–418.
Seikkula, J., & Trimble, D. (2005). Healing elements of dialogue: Therapeutic conversation as an act of love. *Family Process, 44*, 461–475.
Shah, I. (1968). *The way of the Sufi: An anthology of Sufi writings* (p. 205). Penguin Group: New York.
Walsch, N. D. (2005). *The complete conversations with God: An uncommon dialogue.* Charlottesville, VA: Hampton Roads.

Index

A

African American
  beliefs, 53, 54
  church visit, 51
  culture, 53
  faith, 52
  family and community, 50
  poverty and racism, 53
  religion, 54
  slavery, 53
  spirituality, 51, 54
  values, 54
  wisdom, 55

African traditions
  ancestors, 72
  anthropologist and priest, 77
  communal identity, 74
  community, 73
  culture, 73
  heritage, 68
  immigrants, 67, 71
  metaphors, 79
  monotheistic religious traditions, 73
  practices and rituals, 70
  prayers, 77
  refugees, 75
  religion and spirituality, 67
  religious beliefs, 72
  rites of passage, 79, 80
  spirits, 73
  spiritual beliefs, 73
  sun/moon, 73
  worship, 76

Anthrotherapist, 30

Arabs
  belief system, 18, 19
  grief, 23
  immigrated in USA, 27
  internal/external locus of control, 23, 27
  Islamic movement, 17, 28
  Quran, 16
  socialization process, 19
  sociocultural and political, 28
  spiritual practice, 16
  women dress code, 17

B

Bakhtin, M., 125, 126, 131

Balance, 83, 84, 86, 87

Bardos, 12

Beliefs
  African American, 53
  “afterlife”, 25
  Arabs, 18, 19
  hopeful/hopeless, 49
  impermissible, 3
  locus of control, 19
  permissible, 3
  Sikh, 34
  soul, 25
  transcendental meditation, 26

Bibliotherapy, 28

C

Chasidut, 7–9

Chi Gong, 7, 8, 10

D. Trimble (ed.), *Engaging with Spirituality in Family Therapy*, AFTA SpringerBriefs in Family Therapy, https://doi.org/10.1007/978-3-319-77410-7

Christian discourse, 3
Communion, 75–77
Community, 38, 74, 87
Cultural discourses, 45
Culturally relevant intervention
  childhood abuse, 59
  client history, 58
  connectedness, 59
  Energy Psychology, 60
  family story, 59
  hope practices, 61
  psychiatric hospitalizations, 58
  recovery process, 61
  resistance, 59
  sexual trauma, 59
  spirituality, 60
  Spoon Theory, 61
  treatment, 60
Culture, 2, 42
Culture bound syndrome, 108, 119
Cyber infidelity, 28, 29

D
Dialogic practice, 2, 5, 13
Dialogue, 125, 127, 131, 132, 138, 139
Dichotomy, 135
Discourse
  Christianity, 3, 4
  Judaism, 4
  monologue, 4
  neoliberal capitalism, 3, 4
  psychotherapeutic and metaphysical, 7

E
Eastern religion, 85
Energy Psychology, 60
Entanglement, 91
Epigenetics, 90
Epistemology, 42
Ethical practice
  clinical judgment, 6
  informed consent, 7
  metaphysical, 6
  psychotherapeutic principle, 6
  spiritually informed therapy, 6

F
Faith, 57
Faith communities, 38
Faith identities, 34, 35
Family soul, 89–91, 102, 105
Family therapy, 16, 98, 119, 120, 124, 125, 131–132
  Arabs culture (*see* Arabs)
  behavioral change, 57
  hope, faith, and resistance, 57
  questions, 56, 57
  spirituality and religion, 1

G
Global culture, 125, 130, 139
Grief and remedy, 23
Group consciousness, 91, 92, 103

H
Healing systems
  community, 74
  conscious and unconscious ways, 67
  immigrants and refugees, 71–73
  metaphors, 77–79
  prayers, 75–77
  rites of passage, 79, 80
  spiritual foundations, 68–71
Herky–jerky movements, 114
Hindu–Muslim conflict, 37
Hope, 50, 57, 62, 64
  clinical practice, 56, 57
  community-based interventions, 62, 63
  questions, 64
  spirituality and religion, 63
Hopelessness, 49, 50, 62
Humanistic morality, 33
Humanity, 2
Hypertext identity, 41

I
Immigrants, 45, 74
  adaptation, 75
  in Africa, 67
  faithful companioning, 80
  life, 71–73
  refugees (*see also* Refugees)
  spiritual beings, 74
Inclusive theology, 83, 84
Individualism, 125
Instrumental and metaphysical practice, 1, 5, 41, 133
Intergenerational loss, 99–100

Internal/external locus of control, 23, 27
Invisible loyalties, 91
Islamic movement, 17, 28
Islamic spirituality
  "afterlife", 25
  family therapy, 21
  "*Mauled*", 24
  prayers, 23
  Prophet Mohammad, 21
  soul, 25
  transcendental meditation, 26
  trauma, 22

J
Judaism, 4, 5, 7, 8, 12, 21

K
Kabbalah, 7–9, 11, 12
Kakuma refugee camp, 70
Knowing field, 93, 102
Kubler-Ross stage model, 24

L
Language, 18
Learning family therapy, 7
Loss, 21, 23–25, 27
Lost Boys, 74

M
Marriage and Family Therapy, 45
Mental health, 25, 27
Metaphors, 77–79
Monologue, 5
Multiculturalism, 1
Muslim
  politics of religion, 38
  religious identity, 37
  women education, 37

N
Narrative therapists, 43
Narrative therapy, 28
Nature, 84
Negotiated realities, 42, 43
Neoliberal capitalism, 3, 4

O
Obsessive compulsive symptoms, 104–105

P
Palestinians
  Catholic schooling, 20
  modern and traditional lifestyle, 19
  post-trauma, 20
Paradoxical compatibility, 84
Phenomenology, 89
Philosophy, 84, 85
Placebo effect, 17
Polyphonic discourse, 135
Prayers, 22, 23, 26, 75–77
Protestant tradition, 50, 60
Psychotherapeutic practice, 9
Psychotherapy
  benevolent and malevolent spirits, 10, 11
  divorce, 45
  DSM diagnosis, 45
  metaphysical practice, 10, 11
  religion, 39, 40
  self-realization fellowship, 10
  spirituality, 41
  traumatic stress and somatization, 10
  vulnerability, 11
Punjabi Subha movement, 36

Q
Quran therapy
  ritual, 17

R
Reframing, 86
Refugees, 70
  Africa, 75
  children, 74
  immigrants (*see also* Immigrants)
  life, 71–73
  populations, 70
Reiki, 97
Religion in therapy, 4, 39, 40
Religiosity, 27
Religious identity, 34, 37
Religious morality, 33
Resilience, 50, 61, 62, 64
Resistance, 57, 59

Rites of passage, 79, 80
Rivett & Street, 125, 126

S
Sacred space, 12, 13, 39
  ancestors, 124
  appreciation and love, 135
  catastrophic death and destruction, 137
  childlike imaginations, 137
  conversation, 124, 125
  description, 134, 135
  family therapy, 131–132
  in global culture, 130
  imagining, 130
  in-tension, 135
  invitations, 139
  language, 125–129
  location, 132
  pain and suffering, 133–134
  sense of specialness, 136
  spiritans, 129
  spirituality, 124–129, 135
  transcendence, 136
  transformation, 137–139
  video and music, 136
Salat Alistichara ("the guidance seeking prayer"), 26, 27
SANKOFA, 62
  7Cs, 62
  hope, 63
  teaching strategies, 62
  value of connectedness, 63
Segregation, 51, 52
Self, 38, 46
Self-actualization, 108
Self-realization fellowship, 10
Shamanism, 8
Sikh
  belief, 34
  Canadian Sikhs, 36
  discrimination, 40
  divorce, 44
  faith, 36
  gender equity, 44
  political events, 36
  principle, 33
  social inequality, 36
Social inequality, 36
Social justice, 39, 44, 51
Spiritans, 129
Spiritual emergency, 113, 116–119
Spiritual foundations, 68–71
Spiritual identity, 74
Spiritual practice, 46
Spiritual/religious therapy, 17
Spirituality
  agreeing/accepting, 127
  Arabs, 16
  belief systems, 2 (*see also* Beliefs)
  beliefs and practices, 126
  complexity, 126
  conversation, 127
  definition, 54
  experiences, 125
  family therapy, 1
  instrumental and metaphysical interventions, 125
  instrumental practice, 5
  Judaism, 127
  language, 127
  metaphysical practice, 5, 8
  psychotherapy, 3
  religion, 50, 128
  religious tradition, 126
  ritual worship, 128
  socialization, 127
  spiritual communities, 128
Spoon Theory, 61
Sun worshippers, 115
Support Systems and Community Mental Health, 27
Systemic family constellations
  alternative settings, 102–105
  body, mind and spirit connection, 96–98
  church, 96
  clients, 90
  efficacy, 105–106
  family soul, 90
  healing process, 89
  intergenerational loss, 99–100
  intergenerational wounds, 90
  intuition, 89
  invitation, 98
  liturgy, 96
  methods, 92–94
  music, 96
  obsessive compulsive symptoms, 104–105
  origin, 91
  personal history, 94–95
  personal impact, 101, 102
  Reiki, 97
  ripple effect, 103–104
  somatic/personal realms, 89
  spiritual process, 90
  symptom reduction, 90
  systemic thinking, 90
  traditional therapeutic methods, 90

vertigo as teacher, 97
workshop, 99

T
Tao
appealing aspects, 84
clinical constructs, 85–86
community, 87
examination, 84
flow, 87
grace unfolding, 86
Yin and Yang, 85
Taoism
affirming community, 87
appealing aspects, 84
clinical constructs, 85–86
Eastern Philosophy, 85
path, 86
symbolic and spiritual meaning, 84
training, 84
The story of Mot, 74, 75
Transcendence, 84, 136
Transformation, 137–139
Transformational experience, 119
Trans-generational transmission of patterns, 92
Trauma, 22, 24, 27

V
Vertigo, 97
Vision quest
balance, 118
Choctaw and Cherokee tribal people, 110
circumstances, 112
dangerous situations, 110
description, 108
dogma and doctrine, 108
dreams, 110
hope, 109
Lakota, 108
'mysterious tremendum', 109
Native American spiritual experiences, 107
non-tribal people, 108
pastoral setting, 121
planning and reasoning, 109
prayers, 111
revitalization, 118
rituals, 109
self-actualization, 108
spiritual experience, 107
sweat ceremony, 110
sweat lodge ceremony, 111
sweat lodge group, 109
symbols, 119
tribal Sundancers, 108
tribes, 121
united mindfulness, 117
valuable advice, 110
Western concepts, 107
Western Psychological approaches, 107

W
Well-being, 50, 52, 56, 57
Wonders, 136
Writing-in-inquiry, 34, 35, 42